D1563361

YEATS AND THE NOH

Yeats and the Noh

by AKHTAR QAMBER

*with two plays for dancers by Yeats
and two Noh plays*

New York • WEATHERHILL • *Tokyo*

ACKNOWLEDGMENTS

At the Hawk's Well and *The Dreaming of the Bones* reprinted with permission of M. B. Yeats and the Macmillan Companies of London and Canada from *The Collected Plays of W. B. Yeats;* and with permission of The Macmillan Company, New York, from *Collected Plays* by William Butler Yeats, copyright 1934, 1952 by The Macmillan Company.

Hagoromo and *Nishikigi* reprinted by permission of Faber and Faber Ltd., London, from *The Translations of Ezra Pound;* and by permission of New Directions Publishing Corporation, New York, from Ezra Pound and Ernest Fenollosa, *The Classic Noh Theatre of Japan,* copyright © 1959 by New Directions Publishing Corporation.

First edition, 1974

Published by John Weatherhill, Inc., 149 Madison Avenue, New York 10016, with editorial offices at 7–6–13 Roppongi, Minato-ku, Tokyo 106. Copyright © 1974 by Akhtar Qamber; all rights reserved.

LCC 74–84296   ISBN 0-8348-0100-0

Printed in Japan

To my nephew
Kausar

CONTENTS

Author's Preface   11

1. Yeats and the Symbolists   14
2. Irish Theater: The Golden Bridge   23
3. Yeats and the Noh Plays of Japan   37
4. Yeats and the Plays for Dancers   59
5. The Splendor and Sorrows of the Red Branch: About "At the Hawk's Well" and "The Only Jealousy of Emer"   70
6. Evaluation: Hints of a Secret Society   97

Notes to the Text   115

Appendix: Four Plays

At the Hawk's Well, *by* W. B. Yeats   121

The Dreaming of the Bones, *by* W. B. Yeats   131

Hagoromo, *translated by* Ezra Pound and Ernest Fenollosa   142

Nishikigi, *translated by* Ezra Pound and Ernest Fenollosa   147

Bibliography   157

YEATS AND THE NOH

PREFACE

ONE FINE HOLIDAY MORNING, an English friend presented me with a copy of William Butler Yeats's *Last Poems and Plays* with words to this effect: "Here's the latest of Yeats. I've never quite understood the Irish. They are rabid nationalists and believe in fairies under their beds. They are so like you Indians in some respects!"

This last left me gasping for an answer in defense of ourselves, the Indians (we were at that time fighting the British in our nonviolent, Gandhian way and were on the verge of our political independence) or, failing that, in defense of the fairies, at least. For the fact of the matter was that, although this playful generalization was offered in fun, it was very near the truth. I came away thoughtfully with *Last Poems and Plays*.

For one who at that time knew of Yeats only through poems like "The Lake Isle of Innisfree" and "When You Are Old," this was an obscure and disturbing volume. I looked long at the jacket with its depiction of the Egyptian goddess Nut standing on a lion, a starry world held aloft in her long slim hands; the symbol conveyed only vaguely something that, as is appropriate in the case of a symbol, I could not promptly formulate in words. On opening the book I found the poems still more baffling, and cruelly fascinating.

This was the abrupt genesis of my interest in Yeats, beginning with his last poetry and working backward. But not until I took Professor W. Y. Tindall's course on contemporary literature at the Graduate School of Columbia University, New York, did I realize the variety and possibilities of the subject. His lectures opened up new avenues for exploration and filled me with a more than lively zest for Yeats. His gloss and illumination of contemporary texts has been largely responsible for my appreciation of Yeats and has given me an abiding interest in that poet and other modern writers. Also, it was under Professor Tindall's inspiring tutorship that my mind was invigorated and learned the rigors and discipline needed for sustained study and critical scholarship.

Yeats's versatility and large creative range as poet, dramatist, and much else besides leave one no choice but to select one portion of his work on which to focus. His experiment in poetic drama inspired by the classical Noh theater of Japan offers a tidy piece worth dwelling on. In order to realize fully the significance of Yeats's experiment, it is necessary to place it in the ideological setting of his times, in particular that of the symbolist movement as a protest against the scientific humor of the age, and that of the Irish literary renaissance, which, in fact, was one grand aspect of the national consciousness Ireland was experiencing under Parnell's movement for the political liberation of that country.

This dramatic period of Irish history with its wealth of creative energy, Yeats believed, was a suitable time for writers to channel the imagination into dramatic form. Dramatic form for Yeats meant poetic and symbolic drama as against the problem play, social satire, or musical comedy and melodrama of those decades. With his ardor for the aristocracy of intellect, birth, and breeding, Yeats believed in the celebration of all that is high-born, strong, reckless, exceptional. Oisin, Finn, Cuchulain, Usnach's children, Hamlet and Lear, types of Aristotle's "magnanimous man," and "that great rogue Alcibiades" with his extraordinary vitality quickened his imagination. Yeats was frankly partial to heroism, nobility, and chivalry.

As a dramatist he would have felt at home had he been born in the age of Pericles or of Elizabeth I, or the Muromachi period of medieval Japan or the age of Kali Das in ancient India. As a poet, he would have felt particularly blessed, according to his own testimony, had he been permitted to spend even a month "in Byzantium a little before Justinian opened St. Sophia and closed the Academy of Plato."[1]

But as fate would have it, Yeats was born in a materialistic, bourgeois society oppressively dominated by prose and the realistic tradition. His faculty for dream and prophecy, his acute awareness of mystery at the heart of things drove him to an apprehension of reality in nonrealistic terms through the use of myth and symbol, ritual, ceremony, and music: the proper accouterments of a magus and enchanter.

In the realm of dramatic technique, too, Yeats was in search of fresh modes and was moving, as we shall see, toward the style of the courtly Noh drama long before he knew the Noh existed.

I have set myself the following questions, some of which I hope to answer in these pages. Others will bear pondering for a long time.

What was the background of the theater world when Yeats was a young man in search of new ideas and new literary forms?

Why did Yeats have to turn to an East Asian dramatic form when he had behind him and around him the whole rich European tradition, ancient and modern, from Aeschylus to Ibsen and Shaw?

How did he come upon the Noh theater of Japan?

What did he do with it? Was he successful? Better still, was it a rewarding experience to attempt something a little alien, something a little strange, something that was never integrated into the Western dramatic fabric and patterns?

AKHTAR QAMBER

One   YEATS AND
                                        THE SYMBOLISTS

Fresh images beget . . .

WHEN WILLIAM BUTLER YEATS (1865–1939) and his contemporaries
were young men, a strenuous change was taking place in Western
society: in thought, in art, in literature, and in general outlook and
way of life. According to W. Y. Tindall, the three major ideas that
ruled the intellectual and political world of the last quarter of the
nineteenth century came from revolutionary works like Darwin's
Origin of Species (1859), Marx's *Das Kapital* (1867), and the writings
on the new psychology of the unconscious, of dream and association,
advanced by Freud, Jung, and Adler. The works of this group were
published between 1859 and 1887 and made internationally popular
through translations.

    For men of letters there were additional windfalls—philosophies
from India, from lofty works like the *Upanishads,* some of which were
put into matchless English by Yeats, to specious systems like Madam
Blavatsky's version of yoga and her Theosophy. Of particular excitement was the lure of cultures basically different from those of the
West, philosophies of magic and mystery or of repose and simplicity,
with their absence of competition and their unquestioning, resigned

acceptance of tradition. There were also art forms from China and Japan. There were the anthropological studies of Sir James Frazer and Sir Edward Tyler. There were Ibsen, Strindberg, and Maeterlinck, the symbolist movement in France, and, nearer home for Englishmen, the astonishing rhythms and imagery of Gerard Manley Hopkins's new poetry, made available for belated publication through the efforts of his friend Robert Bridges.

One unmistakable note at the turn of the century was that of protest—protest against established religion, social and political institutions, theories of education, bourgeois values in art and language —in short, against the status quo of a civilization marked by hard intellectualism, veneration of both facts and blind faith, materialistic views of life as expressed in serious ambitions for economic prosperity, and the theme of empire. Had it been protest alone, that would have served no end. In the realm of art and literature, at least, there were also the energy and fire of creative genius and a quickened imaginative response to experience. The combination proved significant and generated controversy, experiment, and many aspirations and movements startling but meaningful in the context of the new discoveries.

The refinements and sophistications of the *Savoy* and *Yellow Book* period, of aesthetes like Walter Pater and Oscar Wilde, the sad Ernest Dowson and the shocking Aubrey Beardsley, who were also saying new things in their time, quickly gave way before the more vigorous attempts and aims of the new theater of Ibsen and Shaw, the Irish revival, the symbolist movement, and highly individualistic writers like James Joyce, Ezra Pound, W. B. Yeats, and T. S. Eliot.

By the end of World War I new attitudes and techniques had been fairly well defined; artists and poets had more or less found modes and styles suited to their particular talents and had ranged themselves with the symbolist, realist, naturalist, and other traditions. The period is not without extravagant experiment in the direction of imagism, cubism, vorticism, surrealism, naturalism, and other isms.

Breaking through the late-Victorian tradition in which he had been brought up and against which he was now a rebel, Yeats was reaching out for new and more energetic forms in poetry and drama. He was hunting for a literary manner that would range him opposite realism. The attraction of the symbolist movement for him at this time is undeniable. In his essay "The Symbolism of Poetry," published in 1900, Yeats declared that symbolism was the only movement that was saying new things.

A brief digression on symbolism and Yeats is inevitable here. The symbolist movement, despite French sponsorship, had a continent-wide character and popularity. At the close of the nineteenth century its influence spilled over into England. *The Symbolist Movement in Literature* by Arthur Symons, published in 1899, was largely responsible for disseminating in England the lives and views of European symbolists: Gerard de Nerval, Villiers de l'Isle-Adam, Paul Verlaine, Arthur Rimbaud, Charles Baudelaire, Stéphène Mallarmé, and Maurice Maeterlinck. Several of them, it is said, were living in the border country between mental states of dream and reality, madness and sanity. Their mad moments, no doubt, captured some real insight or bright mood. Even though Yeats and Symons were friends from the time of the Rhymers' Club (roughly 1891–1900), and even though Symons's book on symbolism is dedicated to Yeats, "being the chief representative of that movement in our country,"[1] Yeats owes his inspiration on symbolism only partially to continental writers.

W. Y. Tindall conjectures that Yeats must have come to know the famous play *Axël* by Villiers de l'Isle-Adam between 1890 and 1892. In "Per Amica Silentia Lunae" (1917) Yeats writes: "I had read his *Axël* slowly and laboriously as one reads a sacred book—my French was very bad."[2] Later he saw the play with Maud Gonne on the Paris stage in 1894. The lively synopsis of *Axël* given by Tindall in *Forces in Modern British Literature: 1885–1946* indicates the powerful symbolism of the Rosy Cross and how two lovers "in expiation of their passing infidelity to the spirit of the Rosy Cross and in contempt of the world resolve to die—and die."[3] Not only did Yeats write of *Axël* in at least three essays, "The Autumn of the Body," "Anima Mundi," and "William Blake and the Imagination," but he rewrote his own dramatic poem *The Shadowy Waters* after the manner of *Axël*. Also, the early plays of Maeterlinck, his Belgian contemporary, were regarded by Yeats "as significant protest against the external."[4]

But Yeats seems to have moved away, or rather moved back, from the French to an earlier sphere of influence—to that of esoteric symbolism. In the mid-1880s Yeats became interested in Theosophy. A few years later he joined the Order of the Golden Dawn because of his fascination for the occult, for séances, spiritual mediums, and esoteric rites. MacGregor Mathers, a conspicuous member of the Golden Dawn and a confirmed Celtist, initiated Yeats into many magical practices and rituals. From then on Yeats explored the Kabbala with mounting enthusiasm.

At about the same time, Yeats was writing a study on William Blake, drawn by many affinities to that eccentric mystic and poet. Blake had left a story of violent remonstrance against the mechanistic world-view advanced by Bacon, Locke, and Newton and had striven to preserve intact the integrity of the realm of spirit by the sheer force of his creative imagination. As Professor A. A. Ansari observes in his book on Blake, *Arrows of Intellect,* Yeats was in full sympathy with Blake's way of looking at reality and accorded to Blake's work unchallenged authority. He, with others, felt that art had exhausted the possibilities of description, statement, anecdote, and literal interpretation, in short, of copying from nature. Also, Yeats's temperament responded most readily to the province of the occult, of myth and symbol as adequate ways of suggesting reality and of thinking things out. His essays "Magic," "The Autumn of the Body," and "The Symbolism of Poetry" reveal his belief in what he calls "Anima Mundi," which is a collective reservoir of ancestral and archetypal experiences deposited by the Collective Unconscious of the race. This "Memory of Nature" contains a wealth of images of events, of passions and moods, of memorable personages and wisdom, independent of time and place, of logic and sense-evidence. These images can be revived and evoked by the imagination through symbol, dream, and association of ideas. Yeats believed that the effect of the Great Unconscious upon the conscious life of man, with the ego serving as an intermediary and vital link between the two realms, was unquestionable. It is relevant to quote his doctrine on symbolism from "Magic," written in 1901:

(1) That the borders of our minds are ever shifting, and that many minds can flow into one another, as it were, and create or reveal a single mind, a single energy.

(2) That the borders of our memories are as shifting, and that our memories are a part of one great memory, the memory of Nature herself.

(3) That this great mind and great memory can be evoked by symbols.[5]

There are two primary ways of knowing the world. The bulk of mankind are blessed in that they are content to know it on a matter-of-fact, tangible plane. Others, chiefly artists, are beset by spells of disquiet and brooding over the inexplicable in nature and in man and cannot lay aside their questionings and their wonder despite the pressing fuss and pursuit of daily life. It is not that the phenomenal world ceases to exist for the artist. He recognizes that it is only within the limits of the human and physical that any mind can range and any life be lived. Science has repeatedly satisfied man's curiosity regarding the physical world. Philosophy has tried to satisfy the rational man by imposing order and pattern upon the universe. But man is more than a creature of primary needs. He is more than a rational being. The curiosities and hungers of his whole being at unsuspected levels beyond the physical and the rational can be satisfied, if at all, only by the power and beneficence of the imagination.

Too conscious of the urgency of the "pushing world," Yeats was forever in search of what he called the "enchanted valley." He wrote: "I wanted the strongest passions that had nothing to do with observation and a metrical form that seemed old enough to have been sung by men half asleep or riding upon a journey."[6] Search for the enchanted valley is not an escape. It opens up an additional dimension for living. As Kenneth Burke says: "Literature is not a substitute for action, it is symbolic action."[7] Nor is art in opposition to nature. According to the Platonic doctrine of Divine

Essence, nature itself is a reflection of eternal Forms or Ideas, a mere copy, and an imperfect one, at that. It is true that some art is simply a photographic reproduction of nature, but Plotinus has a pertinent comment on this subject: "Still the arts are not to be slighted on the ground that they create by imitation of natural objects; for, to begin with, these natural objects are themselves imitations; then, we must recognize that they give no bare reproduction of the things seen but go back to the Idea from which Nature itself derives, and further-more, that much of their work is all their own; they are holders of beauty and add where Nature is lacking. Thus Pheidias wrought the Zeus upon no model among things of sense, but by apprehending what form Zeus might take if he chose to become manifest to sight."[8] C. S. Lewis endorses Plotinus's view when he suggests that art may be still another kind of representation of the same eternal reality that nature copies. He writes: "Art and Nature thus become rival copies of the same supersensuous original and there is no reason why art should not sometimes be the better of the two."[9]

The splendor and vitality of the imagination are to be seen in differing ways, as much in the geographical discoveries of the Renaissance sea captains and in Galileo's telescope as in *Hamlet* and *Doctor Faustus;* and in our own day, as much in the celestial voyages of the Geminis and the Apollos as in Gerard Manley Hopkins's "The Wreck of the Deutschland" and Pablo Picasso's *Blue Guitar.* Yeats wanted to reinstate the imagination in some such dazzling, glorious way. As a poet he wanted to re-create reality in the fullest sense—at least in a sense fuller than science does, in a sense that can be received and understood at more levels than one. Recourse to symbolism was therefore a necessity in an age of scientific and factual approaches to life and to complex experience, which especially engages the modern poet's attention. A symbol for Yeats was not a mere decoration or delight or convenience. It expressed the imaginative approach. It was an attempt, as in other ages from Plato onward, to restore the unity of mind and matter, of thought and feeling, of the world of value and the world of fact, through the agency of the imagination, intuitive discernment, and poetic insight.

Myth and symbol, after all, are ways of knowing the world and have been in use from time immemorial. Every culture and religion owns a host of conventional and recognizable symbols, such as the crescent and cross, the staff, serpent, and scrip, the Buddhist stupa, the Indian swastika and *chakra* (wheel). Symbolism has played a vital role in religious experience and artistic activity. Through symbols there can arise a relationship between the spiritual and the material not otherwise discernible or available. Myth and symbol can also throw light on the bewildering aspects of human psychology, mental aberrations and emotional disorders.

As Désirée Hirst points out in her book *Hidden Riches: Traditional Symbolism from the Renaissance to Blake,* the two mainstreams of traditional symbolism tapped by the West derive originally from either Plato or Hebrew mysticism and the Kabbala, the latter represented by generations of Jewish rabbis in their learning and wisdom and in their commentaries on the hidden meaning of the Old Testament and other holy books. In the course of time these influences, passing through the medium of Christian theology and Christian thinking in the works of the Alexandrian Neoplatonists, notably Plotinus (A.D. 204–70), and later the medieval scholastics, harmonized the classical and Christian elements into a fresh composite system.

During the fifteenth century through the Byzantine Neoplatonist Georgius Gemistus (Plethon; 1355–1450), who had been at the Islamic center of Brusa, the Muslim, Persian, and Zoroastrian strains of mysticism also found their way into the Renaissance academies, particularly that of the Medicis at Florence, where Plethon's Italian disciple Marsilio Ficino (1433–99) carried on the good work of translating Plato into Latin and of further reconciling "Platonic philosophy with Christian orthodoxy."[10] It was this complex brand of Neoplatonism that was inherited by Bembo (1470–1547), Castiglione (1478–1529), Ronsard (1524–85), Du Bellay (1522–60), Spenser (1552–99), and Sidney (1554–86). Later, still further modified by the seventeenth-century Cambridge Platonists and by the Swedish mystic Emanuel Swedenborg (1688–1772), with a new symbolic language it was passed on to Blake and thence to Yeats. Both Blake and Yeats subscribed to the philosophical outlook and the conventional symbols of this system as well as invented new symbols out of other experience and knowledge.

Traditional symbols are potent and rich, but for the modern artist who looks upon every experience as unique, symbols have to be freely evolved and so are often arbitrary, intimate, and personal. When ordinary language falls short of communication, the symbol or sign, half revealing and half concealing its meaning, evokes and interprets experience. It presents and confirms the essential reality of psychological states difficult to express in direct discourse and statement. Carlyle's attractive definition comes to mind. He says that "a symbol keeps something silent" and "reveals something eternal." Of course, the danger that the symbol may become entirely silent and obstruct communication has always to be faced, especially in the case of arbitrary or personal symbols that are based on the poet's personal erudition and recondite reading—classical, Biblical, or occult—not accessible to the average reader or accessible to him only at great cost of time and industry.

There is extensive use of symbolism in Yeats's early work, such as *The Wind Among the Reeds, The Countess Cathleen,* and *The Secret Rose,* and in his later, mature volumes, such as *The Tower, The Winding Stair, A Vision* with its elaborate system of symbols, *Four Plays for Dancers,* and *Last Poems and Plays.* Yeats drew upon traditional symbols from Platonism, the Kabbala, and Theosophy and also created his own symbols, such as Byzantium, which stands for wisdom, for "unageing intellect," and for "the artifice of eternity." His heterogeneous system, "his assortment of images" in which some critics find "a certain element of hocus pocus,"[11] suited beautifully both his temperament and his vision of reality.

He believed, as Margaret Rudd says, "that every sensitive man is divided into two, torn between extremes of spirit and matter." Yeats's own "characteristic posture was vacillation. . . . This vacillation to him was the core of the artistic personality"[12] and led him to the theory of the mask, that is, personality as expressed in the self and the antiself, in the mask and the man, in the extrovert, the man of action, and the introvert, the man of contemplation—poet, saint, artist. Yeats writes: "All the gains of man come from conflict with the opposite of his true being.''[13] His philosophy of personality and the inherent poignancy of conflict between opposites are suitable material for drama. They are of the very stuff that is best suggested by symbolic language. As a dramatist Yeats strove to establish a distance from the immediacy of life in order that he might establish a greater intimacy with something within, with some state of mind too intangible for direct statement, and present (not necessarily resolve) the paradoxes and ironies of the human situation that gladden, excite, or make sorrowful the heart of man. Poetic drama, according to him, is such an unfolding of the meaning of external events, and thus it can lay bare the inner situation and often the hidden irrationality through symbol and myth.

The Noh theater of Japan held an irresistible appeal for Yeats, as we shall see, not only for its stylized dramatic technique and its poetic quality, but for its powerful and sustained symbolic representation of action and character.

Before I embark upon the subject of the Noh, however, I would like to turn, in the next chapter, to the English and Irish dramatic environment that made the experiment in the Noh style necessary and possible for Yeats.

Two   IRISH THEATER:
                                  THE GOLDEN BRIDGE

The shaping of an agate . . .

AFTER SEVEN CENTURIES of foreign political domination, nationalist
fervor in Ireland ran high at the end of the nineteenth century and
lasted until the establishment of the Irish Free State in 1922. For
more than forty years Ireland was engaged in a stiff, headlong bid for
national freedom. Political consciousness had been awakened and
encouraged by Parnell's hope of liberating the country through con-
stitutional means. But after the death of this great hero in 1891,
patriotic energy was diverted into other channels, as well. The new
nationalist fervor was partly responsible for rallying the forces of
the imagination that created, among other achievements, the Irish
literary renaissance. It would be equally true to say that nationalist
feeling was quickened and directed by writers like Standish O'Grady
and Sir Samuel Fergusson, who celebrated the heroic age of Finn and
Cuchulain, and George Sigerson and Douglas Hyde, who translated
Gaelic into English and evolved a style at once reminiscent of
"Irish rhythm" and "Irish idiom,"[1] which style was later used by
Lady Augusta Gregory, J. M. Synge, and Father Dineen with great
charm in plays and stories of Irish legend and folklore.
    An interesting parallel between Ireland and Norway is drawn by

23

C. H. Herford in *Beltaine,* an occasional publication like *Samhain* (Yeats's own title for a collection of his writings, chosen for its meaning—"beginning of winter") that ran for a few numbers in 1899 and 1900 with Yeats as editor. In his article "The Scandinavian Dramatists 1840–1860"[2] Herford points out that Henrik Ibsen also grew up during a nationalist revival such as Ireland was experiencing. The modern Scandinavian and the modern Celt have a "heritage of original, magnificent literature of the land," epics and songs of gods and heroes, which are the "stuff of drama." In Norway as in Ireland, nationalism disclosed a "wealth and brilliance" of tradition, and disciplined "vagrant and chaotic enthusiasm" by means of the imagination and artistic invention. The relation of Ibsen to the stirring historical composition of Norway and that of Yeats to Ireland were of a similar nature, though as artists their methods and their creations differed. This divergence may have been due to the difference between the Nordic and Celtic temperaments as well as to differences in individual talent.

In 1851 Ibsen, at the age of twenty-three, became vitally associated with the national theater movement at Bergen and later, in 1857, with the Norwegian theater at Christiania. He valiantly fought his way through long-established Danish dramatic and theater conventions (at that time Denmark's relationship to Norway was similar to that of England to Ireland), until by 1860 he had forged the nucleus of a new drama of first-rate significance that promised to gather European fame and influence.

Partly through nationalist friends like the scholarly John O'Leary, after his long exile in Paris, and Maud Gonne, the political firebrand (and also the most beautiful and spirited lady in the land), but chiefly by reason of his own passionate interest in a literary revival, Yeats became richly involved in the Irish literary movement in its many-sided flowering. From the very beginning he sought to keep sensational politics out of the movement and to stand his ground in spite of political pressure and the general spirit of the times, which was decidedly violent, revolutionary, and unreasoning. He wanted "a new Young Ireland movement like that of Thomas Davis forty years before,"[3] only less active in practical politics and more ambitious for a high standard of excellence in nationalist literature.

With these intentions he founded, in December 1891, the Irish Literary Society in London, and in May 1892 the National Literary Society in Dublin. The first president of the latter was John O'Leary. He was succeeded by Douglas Hyde, whose presidential address, "De-Anglicisation of Ireland," gave rise to the Gaelic League.[4] In the *Irish Quarterly Review* for September 1949, Gerard Murphy, Professor of the History of Celtic Literature at University College, Dublin, in his article "Douglas Hyde" reports that when Hyde was asked by fellow students if he knew Irish, he replied: "I dream in Irish."[5] Hyde thought it a "blighting stigma on nationality" to allow the national language to fall into neglect.

In "Dramatis Personae" Yeats laments that "nothing was read in Ireland except newspapers, prayer-books, popular novels; but if Ireland would not read literature it might listen to it, for politics and the church had created listeners."[6] In his writings on literature the desire for a national theater is repeated again and again. He expressed it as early as the later 1890s to Florence Farr and to Lady Gregory. He reiterated it as late as 1917 in connection with the first performance of *At the Hawk's Well*.

Yeats held two persistent beliefs regarding the theater. The first was "that the Irish people are at that precise stage of their history when imagination shaped by many stirring events desires dramatic expression."[7] Perhaps the imagination turns naturally to the stage in two kinds of historical periods—one, a period in which a nation is passing through crises and hard times on its way to future progress, when the conflict inherent in its situation is in itself dramatic; the other, a period in which a nation wishes to express its sense of splendid achievement and of the human spirit's mastery of environment. In both cases there is the element of tug and thrust that is the foundation of dramatic action. The first is illustrated by the Celtic and the Nordic revivals of the late nineteenth century and the second by the age of Pericles in ancient Greece, the age of Elizabeth in sixteenth-century England, the age of Racine and Molière in seventeenth-century France, and the classical age of Kali Das in fifth-century India.

Yeats's second belief about the theater concerned himself—his belief that his genius, though lyrical, "needed a theatre": "I believe myself to be a dramatist; I desire to show events and not merely tell of them. . . . I seem to myself most alive at the moment when a roomful of people share the one lofty emotion."[8] Yeats believed himself to be a dramatist, whatever the critics might say; and his experience with the Abbey Theatre and contacts with influences from abroad taught him, in the course of years, precisely what kind of theater suited his particular bent and originality.

About one other matter Yeats was certain—that he was in revolt against the English theater of the time. This was not a phase of nationalism. It was, as I understand it, a symptom of a more general reaction against middle and late nineteenth-century industrial and materialistic civilization, the tyranny of which was acutely felt everywhere in Europe and Britain by men of sensitivity and independence of mind.

In the field of drama the English and the Irish followed separate lines of development. "The Anglo-Saxons, having conquered the world of matter," as Cazamian puts it in *A History of English Literature,* proceeded to use their discoveries concerning the nature of man—his emotions, his psychology, the limitations and fruits of environment and heredity, and the laws that govern society—to deal with modes of living in organized groups in a mechanized age. Since the successful, vivacious comedy of Goldsmith and Sheridan (both, incidentally, of Irish origin), drama had languished and all but died. The literary genius of the nineteenth century, on the other hand, threw itself with zest into lyric, novel, essay, and controversy. But in the last quarter of the century, through the devotion of Edmund Gosse, William Archer, and George Bernard Shaw, Ibsen's inspiration was to bring renewed energy, excitement, and stamina to the English stage.[9] Bold characterization, vigorous dialogue, realistic stage representation in setting and in costume, and the discussion of pressing contemporary problems became the main concerns and ideals of English playwrights. Galsworthy and Shaw, two of the most prominent playwrights of the period, writing in the manner of

Ibsen, nevertheless could not depict conflict among the essential passions and impulses of human nature the way Ibsen could. They portrayed social content more than human.

Galsworthy and Shaw were passionately interested in contemporary society—the business and ethics of living in organized social units. Yeats complained that Shaw was occupied with propaganda and reform and Galsworthy with serious debates and lawsuits. Neither did Oscar Wilde's brilliant and scintillating comedy of British high society, in a class by itself, appeal to him. Nor for that matter did the fantasy of James Barrie and the dozens of other popular nineteenth-century dramatic genres. Yeats believed that a playhouse was a place for "intellectual excitement and not a platform" for social satire and practical concerns. Perhaps the intellectual climate of England at the time was too dry and uncongenial for a good play, poetic or realistic, in spite of the attempt to import Ibsen's model for drama, so full of possibilities in the north of Europe.

Examining the Celtic temperament and psychology, we find that the traditional "Celtic mind is all made up of melancholy, emotion and mysticism."[10] Speaking of the Irish storyteller, Yeats says: "His imagination was always running off to Tir-nà nOg, to the land of promise . . . always athirst for emotion, a beauty which cannot be found in its perfection upon earth, or only for a moment. . . . His art, too, is often at its greatest when it is most extravagant, for he only feels himself among solid things, among things with fixed laws and satisfying purposes, when he has reshaped the world according to his heart's desire."[11]

The "Irish traditional temperament" inclines to brooding imagination and disquieted "wanderings of the will." However, it also has "flashes of clear-sighted and matter-of-fact realism."[12] The combination results in a special quality of poetic vision. A genuine visionary must have his feet firmly planted on the earth; otherwise his prophecy and his dream have no foundation to build on and therefore sound unreal and are unconvincing. By this I do not propose to exalt all Irishmen, or even all Irish poets, to the level of seers; but it should be noticed that Yeats's mind was enriched by the above qualities fused with those gained by contact with England and France. In him there is a blending of strong intellectual fiber with a heightened sensibility and imagination.

Yeats was dissatisfied with the existing theater on still another score: stagecraft. The London theater appeared to him crudely realistic, seeking mere clarity of statement. In "The Irish Dramatic Movement: 1901–1919" he writes that "Ibsen has sincerity and logic beyond any writer of our time, . . . [but] lacks beautiful and vivid language."[13] To be fair to Ibsen, it must be said that only one aspect of his drama featured realistic representation. Una Ellis-Fermor in her book *The Irish Dramatic Movement* draws attention to the fact that the phase of Ibsen which, after the first shock of novelty, became popular in England was that of the problem play or the play of social satire. William Archer's translation of *Pillars of Society* was performed in 1880, and by 1888 translations of such plays as *Ghosts* and *An Enemy of the People* had sold well. However, Edmund Gosse had discovered *Brand* and *Peer Gynt* as early as 1872. These latter plays are of intense lyrical beauty, searching the soul of man and his inner tragedy through the sustained and powerful symbolism of their central characters, Brand and Peer. It would be an interesting speculation to consider the effects on the English stage and on Yeats if *Peer Gynt* and *Brand* had been popularized in England before the play of ideas, such as *A Doll's House* and *Ghosts*. As matters stand, according to Yeats, realism produces a dead and abstract language. He characteristically sums up: "All language but that of the poet and of the poor is already bed-ridden."[14]

Yeats has further quarrels with the English stage: It flatters the taste of the middle class and is sadly commercialized. Drama has become a travesty of the life of the rich and "impoverishes the imagination." Instead of Lear and Cordelia there are actual millionaires, who, it is hoped, "will soon be robbed and murdered." Again, "drama is a moment of intense action" and should be freed from preoccupation with morals and reform in the narrow sense. He thinks that Shaw's comedies are less than life because Shaw is a reformer. "Mr. Wilde could hardly finish an act of a play without denouncing the British public." George Moore "has not for ten years now been able to keep himself from the praise and blame of the Church of his fathers."[15] What chance, laments Yeats, has "the living imagination" in such a world?

Edward Martyn in his "Comparison Between English and Irish Theatrical Audience" in *Beltaine*[16] is even more extreme. He finds nothing enlightened or refined in a civilization when a poet like "Kipling is the voice of the nation." He maintains that contemporary England is choked with outworn systems, and that English influence on Ireland is bad. "No two countries and no two languages blend worse together." Both Edward Martyn and George Moore express their ideas on the theater vehemently and foretell the fall of the British empire. The Romans in their decline were satisfied with the arena, they observe; the British enjoy musical comedy and variety shows. "Artistic intelligence in England has dwindled in the last twenty years," says Moore in an article called "Is the Theatre a Place for Amusement?" It seeks distraction such as the circus and the race-course provide. It does not seek pleasure, which is defined by Moore as the "rousing of yourself out of the lethargy of real life."[17]

In Ireland the intellectual awakening was founded on idealism. The poetry implicit in the ancient traditions of the land and that inspired by the new contemporary struggle were the "golden bridge" (Yeats's phrase in *The Celtic Twilight*) on which the Irish theater was built. "A good play," said Moore, "was possible in Dublin." In 1900 Yeats was still very uncertain regarding the possibilities of the theater. He doubted that great literature could come out of Ireland yet. But he believed that the Irish people had been roused spiritually and morally because of their experiences of political struggle and their sacrifices. Some kind of awakening was at hand.

Yeats's *Cathleen ni Houlihan*, played for the first time with Irish actors in 1902 (with Maud Gonne, it is said, acting magnificently the part of Cathleen), embodied just such a symbol of Ireland. The heroine, a queenly old peasant woman who looks like a young girl, rouses the young to commit themselves to the cause of Irish political freedom and to make sacrifices for the motherland.

But it must not be thought for a moment that all was plain sailing in Ireland. The Irish Literary Theatre was founded in 1899 by Yeats, Martyn, Moore, and Lady Gregory. After three seasons Moore and

Martyn dropped out, leaving Yeats with mingled feelings of loss and freedom. There were differences of opinion on matters of realism and prosaic language. Martyn was also disturbed by the bitter attack Yeats's *Countess Cathleen* had received from the Catholic church. It was averred that Yeats had sold Cathleen's soul for worldly gain and then contrived to secure salvation for the sinner on grounds of motive. A little later, J. M. Synge's *Playboy of the Western World* was also attacked by puritanical opinion. Yeats engaged in fiery controversy over *Playboy,* clarifying to the public his ideas on morality. He defended the play in a debate on February 4, 1907, at the Abbey Theatre, for by this time the Irish Literary Society had acquired a playhouse of its own. He did not wish it to be thought that he denied the moral principle in literature. He believed with the Belgian poet Emile Verhaeren that "a masterpiece is a portion of the conscience of mankind,"[18] but his moral sense was far from being identical with that of the pulpit or the press. Another controversy erupted over Synge's *Shadow of the Glen,* this time with the extreme nationalist party, and Yeats took the opportunity to show what he thought constituted a national theater and how much he mistrusted literature with a political flavor. Yeats felt that "drama with an obviously patriotic intention . . . could have roused opinion; but . . . could not have touched the heart."[19]

It would be highly diverting to relate the dramatic story of the Irish theater movement; but while space will not permit this, the story of the founding of the Abbey Theatre and the gifted personalities connected with it are so irresistible that I am compelled to digress for a bit.

The present Abbey Theatre in Lower Abbey Street, Dublin, was built in 1966 after the original had burned down in 1951. The new theater, designed by the Irish architect Michael Scott, seats 628 in the main theater and 160 in the smaller Peacock Theatre, meant only for verse plays and poetry readings.[20] The original Abbey Theatre stood on the same site and was founded in 1904 through the good offices of the English patron Annie Horniman, who graciously gave funds for the building from her shares in the Hudson's Bay Company, in which her family were tea magnates. She left, however, not so graciously, over a quarrel with Yeats, Synge, Lady Gregory, and the Fay brothers and established a rival theater—the repertory Gaiety Theatre in Manchester. Lady Gregory's support and inspiration were far more consistent and enduring. Her role in the Irish theater movement was of an intellectual order. She was a writer in her own right and had fine discrimination and taste. She did much to further the Celtic cultural renaissance. Her book *Cuchulain of Muirthemne* is beautifully written and shows her feeling and sensitivity for the Irish heritage of the heroic age.

Quite the most striking among the writers was George Moore. He often sacrificed the serious aspect of a situation or character because, like Shaw, he could not resist the comic moment. He was ever ready for collaborative writing, meddling with other people's texts and full of interesting ideas on play writing and play acting. No sooner had he joined than he left the theater project, and none too soon. Lady Gregory was apprehensive lest his ideas on style prove injurious to Yeats's style. Moore's cousin Edward Martyn, "the peasant saint" as Yeats affectionately called him, withdrew himself and his money almost before he joined the group, partly because he was intimidated, as was suggested above, by clerical assaults on the new theater.

The Fay brothers, Frank and Willie, who were in Dublin till 1908, were distinguished for their fine acting under the direction of Lennox Robinson. Yeats, who had been looking for voices suited to verse drama, at last found one in Florence Farr. "Miss Farr . . . has . . . the most beautiful voice on the English stage and is, in her management of it, an exquisite artist."[21] Yeats said he had "never heard verse better spoken than by [her]." (At the age of fifty she could still speak Yeats's poems to the accompaniment of the psaltery.) With a voice like hers, verse drama became possible. Yeats found a comparable male voice in Frank Fay—"that speech of his, so masculine and so musical."[22]

Florence Farr, moreover, was an accomplished actress and had played major roles in Shaw's *Widowers' Houses* and *Arms and the Man* and in Yeats's *Land of Heart's Desire, The Countess Cathleen,* and *The Shadowy Waters. The Land of Heart's Desire* and *Arms and the Man* were written for Florence Farr. Richard Bax, who edited *Florence Farr, Bernard Shaw, W. B. Yeats: Letters,* pays a grand tribute to Florence Farr when he says that "she was, in fact, one of the four or five genuinely poetic women whom I have known."[23] In the women's gallery one must not forget Sarah Bernhardt, with her haunting voice, and Sara Allgood, another talented actress.

Not the least among these celebrities were the playwrights themselves and those who designed stage settings and costumes and wrote or arranged music for the plays. Altogether it must have been a brilliant circle, with charm of personality and exciting and daring new theories on the theater in general and the role and function of the Abbey Theatre in particular. But it is of more immediate concern to continue with Yeats's principles and views on drama.

The relation of drama to morality, nationalism, and the middle class has already been touched upon. Something further must be said on the technique of play writing and stage representation in poetic drama, and it must be pointed out how from the very early beginnings Yeats was gravitating toward the ideals of the Noh stage of Japan, which he was to come to know later. The following ideas are gleaned from material found in *Beltaine, Samhain, Dramatis Personae,* and *Plays and Controversies,* where Yeats has repeated himself amply. The repetition is evidence enough of the force and tenacity with which he believed in his ideas.

He believed that "the theatre [is] a place of intellectual excitement," not a platform for propaganda; that drama is essentially literature; that literature "describes the relation of the soul and the heart to the facts of life and of law"; that it represents "life, which in its essence is always surprising, always taking some new shape, always individualising." It has nothing to do with regimentation, uniformity, types, "men moving in squads."[24]

Their partiality to naturalism, topical situations, and realistic characters was one of the main reasons why George Moore and Edward Martyn left the Irish Literary Society. There was a little tug of war over *Diarmuid and Grania,* a prose play on which Yeats and Moore had collaborated unsuccessfully. Moore's dramas, Yeats bewailed, were "about possible people. . . . He insisted for days upon calling the Fianna 'soldiers'. . . . He made the dying Diarmuid say to Finn, 'I will kick you down the stairway of the stars.' "[25] Only in wishing to escape artificiality and sham was Yeats at one with the Ibsenites Shaw and Archer. In the section in *Explorations* entitled "The Irish Dramatic Movement: 1901–1919" he resents the fact that "the preoccupation of men with all kinds of practical changes has driven the imagination out of the world. . . . The creative energy of men depends on their believing that they have within themselves something immortal and imperishable and that all else is but an image in a looking-glass."[26] Poetic drama must keep a distance from daily life so that it may keep the force and poetry of its emotion. "It is only by extravagance, by an emphasis far greater than that of life, as we observe it, that we can crowd into a few minutes the knowledge of years."[27]

Another important matter Yeats discusses again and again is style. Sainte-Beuve's dictum "There is nothing immortal in literature except style"[28] was full of significance for Yeats. He knew the magic of "sentences men murmur again and again for years." He admired Douglas Hyde's Gaelic dialect, "spontaneous, joyous, . . . every speech born out of itself." He believed that the Irish have a natural genius for speech. There is no need to leave Ireland to learn dialogue. Yeats quotes a relative who wrote to him the following: "It is natural to an Irishman to write plays; he has an inborn love of dialogue and sound about him; of a dialogue as lively, gallant and passionate as in the times of great Eliza."[29] This Irish claim reminds one of Oscar Wilde and George Bernard Shaw, brilliant talkers whose sense of paradox and irony could throw such a spell on the reader or playgoer that if these writers had so chosen they could have compelled sense out of sheer nonsense. Both Farquhar and Goldsmith were Irish, and Congreve was brought up in Ireland. They could all talk—they were masters of dialogue.

In drama, Yeats's emphasis is on speech, on the spoken word, which he considers more important than gesture. The chanting of verse is far better than "broken attempts at realism." Recitals and declamations must be avoided at all costs. Not only must words be beautiful, appropriate, and suggestive, but they must be spoken in a clear and simple way. The rhythm and cadence of speech must be palpable in the voice. Yeats was attempting to revive the ancient art of minstrelsy. As has been pointed out already, in Florence Farr he had found an "accomplished speaker of verse."[30] He would capture anyone who had a good speaking voice. It is said that the young girl who played the part of the fairy child in The Land of Heart's Desire pleased him tremendously.

Yeats was equally taxing and meticulous about acting. Actors must "keep still enough to give poetical writing its full effect upon the stage." A few simple significant movements were enough. His description of the acting of Sarah Bernhardt and De Max in Phèdre is relevant. Yeats noticed great "periods of stillness" that were partially unintentional, for the inexperienced "actors did not know what else to do," but these intervals pleased him. "Their gestures had a rhythmic progression. . . . Sarah Bernhardt would keep her hands clasped over, let us say, her right breast for some time, and then move them to the other side, perhaps lowering her chin till it touched her hands, and then, after another long stillness she would unclasp them and hold one out, and so on, not lowering them till she had exhausted all the gestures of uplifted hands. . . . De Max was quite as fine. . . . The white-robed men never moved at all. . . . The whole scene had the nobility of Greek sculpture and an extraordinary reality and intensity."[31] Yeats goes on to say that he understood, then, Goethe's dictum "Art is art because it is not nature."

Yeats also had pronounced ideas regarding costumes, makeup, and scenery. The backdrop is to be looked upon not as a landscape but as the canvas of a portrait, with a single color and shadows to suggest mountains or rivers. Scenery is to be unobtrusive so that the imagination of the audience is not distracted and is free to create scenes[32] and habitations according to each viewer's own artistic conception. A single tree can suggest a forest or shade more effectively than can a realistic forest.

Despairing of the proper use of makeup, Yeats was all for abandoning it altogether and using masks instead. The problem of costumes also occupied his attention. These matters will be considered at greater length in the discussion of his plays for dancers.

If I have interpreted Yeats's ideas on drama aright, I would say that everything in him is tending toward two things: imagination and artistry. He speaks of imaginative energy repeatedly. The imagination is coming into its own. He observes in *Explorations* that the "hour of convention, decoration and ceremony is coming again." Poetry alone is to redeem the theater and "by its impact help to preserve the distance from daily life."[33]

The essence of Yeats's theory of distance and intimacy in the theater lies in his antagonism to the realistic approach in literature and drama so popular in his day. The "distance from daily life" of which he writes again and again he achieves through subject, theme, and attitude on the one hand and style and dramatic technique on the other. The ancient mythological figures of Irish legend—Cuchulain, Emer, and others—that Yeats uses in many of his plays are literally distant in time. In addition these personages, though human like the rest of us in their pursuit of love, youth, beauty, and brave deeds and in their experiences of death and suffering, are yet exceptional in that they live on a grand, heroic, romantic plane. This gives them another kind of remoteness from daily life.

Again, the treatment of their experiences is not through discursive language and direct discourse but through symbol, poetic language, and poetic imagery, all of which are capable of suggesting echoes and reverberations of meaning, and inward states of mind, and of eliciting complex emotional responses. Thirdly, the stylized marionettelike movements, the use of masks, music, and chanting of verse that distinguish their stage production give these plays by Yeats an atmosphere of ritual, remoteness, and reverie very different from that of the realistic drama of political propaganda and social problems.

Yet, paradoxically, the very factors of artifice and imagination that lend these plays distance from daily life make a primary and immediate appeal to the hearts and minds of the audience. In this way, the timeless, universal experiences of the plays—experiences that are the lot of all men—become still more personal, more intimate, more deeply moving. The response to these plays is like that to the poetry of passion and beauty. Furthermore, the physical smallness of the theater, which was very important to Yeats, creates literal intimacy. Lastly, in Yeats's words, "a roomful" of like-minded, chosen playgoers "share the one lofty emotion" in a strangely psychologically intimate way.

From 1900 on, Yeats was seeking to create a distinctive and fresh dramatic form in which the aristocrat, the peasant, and the poet, imagination, song, and ritual were to play a leading role. He wrote, spoke, debated, and experimented with his theories for the next twelve years or more. With the support and sympathy of friends like Douglas Hyde, who could use Gaelic rhythmic patterns; devoted actors like the Fay brothers, Florence Farr, and Sarah Bernhardt; and above all Lady Gregory with her love of poetry, her zeal for Ireland, and her aristocracy presiding over the whole scene, Yeats was able to hold firmly to his convictions. It seemed he might be very near to building the theater of his imagination and to giving expression to his nostalgia for Lears and Cordelias, for legendary heroes, saints, and peasants, for noble action and poetic speech.

Then, as magically as all good things happen, Yeats met Ezra Pound and by a happy trick of fate discovered the classical Noh theater of Japan.

Three

YEATS AND THE
NOH PLAYS OF JAPAN

To lords and ladies of Byzantium . . .

BEFORE WORLD WAR II Ezra Pound was an interesting and forceful figure in the lives of artists, scholars, and literary men. In the discomfiting story of the publication of *Ulysses,* James Joyce relates how "my friend Ezra Pound and good luck brought me into contact with . . . Sylvia Beach . . . a brave woman, who risked what professional publishers did not wish to,"[1] with the result that on his fortieth birthday, February 2, 1922, Joyce received the first printed copy of the "voluminous manuscript of *Ulysses,*" which must have peregrinated the streets of Paris with its creator since 1920.

Earlier, Pound had been bent on other errands of mercy. "He had breezed into England in 1908," writes Richard Ellmann, "confident and full of information about obscure literature . . . and was busy from the time of his arrival in separating both living and dead poets into the readable and the unreadable."[2] He must have first met Yeats sometime between 1908 and 1912. In 1912 he had annoyed Yeats by altering, without permission, some verses that had been entrusted to him for the magazine *Poetry.*[3] But after this little episode his benefactions to Yeats were many and varied. In *A Packet for Ezra Pound* Yeats acknowledges that Pound taught him how to fence, and read aloud to him when Yeats's eyesight was bad. Yeats writes: "I shall not soon forget the rehearsal of the *Hawk's Well* when Mr. Ezra Pound, who had never acted on any stage, in the absence of our chief player, rehearsed for half an hour."[4] Pound also encouraged Yeats to change his style of verse writing. Being an ardent imagist, Pound believed in spare, exact, and sharply defined language. Nothing came of the fencing, but Yeats's writing style became more and more robust, stripped of ornament and increasingly precise as time went on. Pound's influence on T. S. Eliot's *The Waste Land* was of a similar kind.

During the winters of 1913–14, 1914–15, and 1915–16 Pound acted as Yeats's secretary at Ashdown Forest in Sussex. In 1913 Pound also became the literary executor of Ernest Fenollosa, who for many years had been a student of Chinese and Japanese art and literature.[5] The "obscure literature" mentioned above was nothing other than the manuscripts of Fenollosa and Pound. At that time Pound was working on these, among them Fenollosa's draft translations of Noh plays of Japan, which were published presently in English magazines like *The Quarterly Review, Poetry,* and *Drama.* The publication of four of the Noh translations, *Hagoromo, Nishikigi, Kumasaka,* and *Kagekiyo,* by the Cuala Press in 1916 in a volume entitled *Certain Noble Plays of Japan,* selected and edited by Ezra Pound and with an introduction by W. B. Yeats, was an exciting literary event. Hopefully, 350 copies were printed. The same year Macmillan published another notable volume, *'Noh' or Accomplishment: A Study of the Classical Stage of Japan,* by Fenollosa and Pound. This contained fifteen Noh translations, including the above four.

Pound, again with his characteristic genius for discovering exceptional people, in 1915 discovered the talented Japanese dancer Michio Ito, then living in indigence and obscurity in London.[6] Yeats was delighted to meet Ito and to procure his services until the young dancer was whisked away by the New York theater, which had swooped down on the Abbey Theatre before and carried away actors like Dudley Digges. As Gerard Fay rightly complains, Broadway and Hollywood still carry away promising talent from the Abbey Theatre.[7] Yeats also met Arthur Waley, a scholar of Chinese and Japanese, and Gordon Craig, son of Ellen Terry, who had been trained under Henry Irving and who initiated Yeats into the effects of stage lighting.[8] He also met Edmund Dulac, who wrote music and designed costumes for Yeats's plays; in 1918 he made a woodcut of Giraldus Cambriensis that is now found in *A Vision*.

One can well imagine the excitement of Yeats at this timely succession of events and at the discovery of these gifted people and of an ancient art that seemed to embody the noblest ideals of his dream for the Irish stage. Aristocracy, symbolism, ritual, beautiful words were all here in the Noh theater, combined in a magic of artful creation. One is sorely tempted to compare Yeats to the merchant in the Bible "who when he had found one pearl of great price sold all that he had and bought it," but the comparison would not be wholly just. For one thing, Yeats was an experimenter and kept an open mind, eager to try whatever took his fancy and whatever seemed to extend the boundaries of art. The same spirit of inquiry and trial had informed his other absorptions, such as Theosophy, the Kabbala, symbolism, Blake, the Celtic revival—and later automatic writing and the new philosophy of civilizations and of personality. For another, he was forced to return to his earlier European dramatic tradition in plays like *The Words upon the Window-Pane, The Resurrection,* and *Purgatory.* But while the phase of the Noh lasted, it brought choice and fruitful results in the volume entitled *Four Plays for Dancers.* Yeats wrote that he regretted not having discovered the Noh earlier.

At this point it becomes necessary to introduce the Noh theater of Japan. But first a word in general about the Japanese aesthetic sensibility and some dominant principles that underlie traditional Japanese art forms, particularly monochrome ink painting, dry-landscape gardens, *bonsai* (dwarfed trees), *ikebana* (flower arrangement), and the most sophisticated, the most eccentric of the arts—the tea ceremony and the courtly Noh theater.[9] Interestingly enough, Japanese artistic traits find expression not only in the arts; often they are also reciprocated in the Japanese way of life; that is, at many points life and art are governed by the same principles, the same self-consciousness, refinement, and ceremony. For instance, the Japanese artistry and sense of formality extend equally to a pedestrian act like wrapping a parcel in a modern department store and to the ritual of holding a tea bowl at the snobbishly aloof tea ceremony.

The outsider is not a little impressed by the Japanese propensity for imitation, and indeed the charge is confirmed by the swift progress Japan has made in the know-how of Western science and technology since the Meiji Restoration in 1868. Earlier in Japanese history, from about A.D. 552 to the end of the eighth century, there was heightened traffic on all fronts between China and Korea on the one hand and Japan on the other. Under princely patronage beginning with Prince Shotoku (574–622), well-chosen scholars and diplomatic embassies brought back to Japan the arts and sciences of the continent. China of the T'ang dynasty held a magical fascination for the new and rising Japanese rulers. They imported vigorously and lavishly the Chinese imperial concept of government, the Chinese plan of rectangular cities laid out in a grid pattern, Chinese administration, the burdensome Chinese script, and above all the Chinese Mahayana and Zen forms of Buddhism. Of these the Zen school has had an especially profound influence on Japanese philosophy and on Japanese classical arts.

The paradox that meets one here is that despite initial borrowings and foreign cultural gains the Japanese have created, over many centuries in their island home shut off from the rest of the world, an uninterrupted and distinctively Japanese civilization. There is something unique about their houses, their interior decoration, their temple and garden architecture, their arts and crafts, their dress, and their food.

During these same twelve centuries the genteel, debonair Chinese tradition gave way to the tougher spirit of the Japanese warrior class, which as custodian of the land during the medieval period developed the much-cherished martial qualities of alertness, courage, pride, loyalty, and indifference to suffering. The Japanese stoicism in the face of death and personal loss is difficult to understand and almost impossible to emulate. In addition, as Edwin O. Reischauer observes in *Japan Past and Present,* the warriors, obsessed with strenuous wars and the futility of battlefield honors and glory, were driven to the austere philosophy of Zen Buddhism. Six hundred years of Spartan living and attitudes created the national character and gave rise, among other things, to the most meditative and most symbolic of the Japanese arts—the tea ceremony and the Noh.

But more than China and Korea and the modern West, nature has been the Japanese artist's most loved and persistent teacher. Not that art and nature are ever identical. The terms "imitation of nature" or "reproduction of nature" cannot with any justice be used here unless they are used insofar as every artist, Japanese or otherwise, must of necessity learn from his natural and human environment. In fact Japanese art is created with such deliberate intention, such reverence for tradition, and such fidelity to individual vision that it is unmistakably art and not nature. The artist's exuberant energy and his spontaneity are severely controlled in the selection and ordering of the material offered by nature's profusion, its eternal patterns, its laws and behavior. It is routine to see schoolchildren with paints, brushes, and canvas let loose upon some scene of natural beauty and wonder and systematically exposed (like Wordsworth's Lucy) to whatever influences may be abroad among the woods, sands, and hills. The largest number of tourists who "do the sights," I noticed during my stay in Japan, were not the moneyed foreigners but the Japanese themselves. Men and women armed with cameras visit the famed cities of Kyoto, Nara, Kamakura, Nikko, Tokyo, Osaka. They hike in the Japan Alps, bathe in the steaming hot springs of Izu and Atami. Multitudes set out daily to view cherry blossoms in the windy month of April, and to view autumn foliage in the fall; and in all seasons the viewing of Mount Fuji, ever changing in light and shade, yet ever the same, is a joyous national pastime.

This is not to be wondered at. Japan's natural endowments and scenic beauty are breathtaking. Despite typhoons and earthquakes, the setting is soft and enchanting. Living in the "divine country where grew the herbs of eternal life"—with its myriad rocky islands in the blue Pacific, its enchanted and enchanting Inland Sea, its choice collection of mountains, lakes, and white rolling beaches, the wealth and nobility of its forests of cedar, maple, pine, oak, and cypress —it would be disappointing if the Japanese were not artistic. If their reputation in this area is exaggerated at all, it is less exaggerated than the Indian reputation for being spiritual! With artistic talent the Japanese combine the artistic temperament. By this I mean that their attitude to life contains a strong element of this-worldliness. They are not naturally world-renouncing or world-weary. It was the generous, compassionate Mahayana expression of Buddhism that appealed to them more than the ascetic Hinayana form of the religion. The Japanese believe that the ghosts of their ancestors return to haunt the scenes of earthly life. It is hard for them to renounce beautiful Japan. Thus the Japanese imagination tends toward concrete images and art forms rather than toward metaphysics and abstractions.

Secondly, though nature in Japan is prodigal of beauty, the Japanese artist is drawn toward the beauty of "solitariness." The discipline of picking out needed elements from the chaos and formlessness of the material at his disposal is his chief forte. Reticence is a prominent principle in art as in life. A solitary flower in a vase is not an uncommon sight. The multifoliate expression of the Indian imagination as seen in the sun temples at Konarak and Puri and the austerity of Japan's Ise Shrine present an arresting contrast. Each is great in its own place. In the renowned dry-landscape garden of the Zen temple Ryoan-ji in Kyoto, more symbolism than garden, fifteen stones of selected shape and size are so arranged in a setting of white raked sand that no matter where one stands, at least one stone seems always missing. This teasing "scanty exhibition" yields infinite scope for meditation and intellectual delight. The Japanese conventional poetic forms, the seventeen-syllable *haiku* and the thirty-one-syllable *waka,* are characterized by the same extreme economy.

Formal expressions and honorific address the Japanese have in plenty. In politics, where talk hides more than it reveals, and in the intimacy of the family circle, the Japanese are as vocal as people anywhere; but polite conversation is marked by frugality. A sentence with the mere hint of a compliment or reproach will conveniently remain unfinished, suggesting many unsaid, tantalizing, exhilarating possibilities. My Japanese students used to answer examination questions with stunning brevity. The only Chinese boy I had in my classes seemed to them unnecessarily expansive. I used to wonder what they

would think of our Indian gift of tongues—of Radhakrishnan's elo-
quence and Nehru's discursiveness. From the time of the *Upanishads*
we Indians have been fluent in describing, defining, explaining,
arguing, debating, and with clarity, charm, and winsomeness, too.
The Japanese believe in few words—in solitariness and astringency.
This is beauty of another kind.

Allied traits are sobriety and unobtrusiveness, which stem from
the Shinto and Zen traditions. In color and outline the Japanese re-
ject boldness, gaiety, and glamor. Their favorite shades are nature's
own blues and grays and browns and greens. The vivacity and brightness of vermilion, gold, and purple, and the Chinese-style deco-
rations of Nikko, the most popular of the historical shrines with
foreigners, are embarrassing to traditional Japanese taste. The Japanese would find it immensely exciting to discover a temple or a house
modestly camouflaged in wooded surroundings.

But the most outstanding principle of Japanese art is asymmetry.
The "fearful symmetry" Blake found in the tiger and which the visi-
tor to Japan finds in the august spectacle of Mount Fuji are rare ac-
complishments and can come only from the hand of God. Man can
only dream of and evoke images of perfection. In real life the pattern
of experience begins, breaks, and falls apart before one has seen it
anywhere near completion. The Japanese artist recognizes the myth
of perfection in earthly life and articulates that wisdom by presenting
a partial view of reality. For instance, the chief architectural motif
of the main building of Nijo Castle in Kyoto is repeated only in a
smaller wing on the viewer's left, with nothing to balance it on the
right. To those of us who are accustomed to, say, identical rows of
evergreens and roses in a Mughal garden, the vacancy on the right is
disturbing, as is the pairing of a tangerine and a cherry tree at the
entrance of the Imperial Palace in Kyoto. A Japanese garden, especially a teahouse garden, is a masterpiece of unpredictability. It
presents no open, straightforward, static picture that we can hold
in the mind. In a minimum of space, the garden presents an illusion
of size and depth that change with the position of the beholder.
The beholder is always asked to view the garden from certain
specified spots that yield the greatest diversity and pleasure. The

gardener is at pains to preserve two feelings: *sabi,* the feeling of hoariness, ancientness, strength, and permanence; and *wabi,* the feeling of tranquillity and repose, even melancholy. Seasonal garden plants and flowers, which bloom and fade, are considered a painful reminder of the short-lived quality of human experience.

Again, the Japanese artist believes that nature's ugly, deformed, and frail aspects can teach man sympathy and tenderness for the distortions and abnormalities from which they suffer and which should create pity in the heart of man, thus tempering and restraining the Japanese spirit of strife and covetousness. It is only the tall, the well-formed, and the pleasing object that excites envy. There are two special words in Japanese to represent these concepts. *Furyu* means the feeling of tenderness, humility, and quiet enjoyment. *Bushido,* "the way of the warrior," means the spirit of competition and the love of possession and mastery. The horticultural art of dwarfing trees is an excellent study in the grotesque and is an extension of *furyu.* I have seen a six-hundred-year-old dwarfed oak tree no taller than two feet. But it bore all the signs of old age and of the botanical evolution natural to it in the course of those six hundred years.

To lay out a garden, to engage in the tea ritual, to witness the Noh are said to be acts of *furyu,* and the exercise partakes of the qualities of contemplation and of communion with the divine. These Zen-influenced arts are the products of infinite patience, concentration, self-consciousness, and, of course, leisure. They help to establish a distance from life, as Yeats would have said, and teach one the concepts of nonattachment and repose of mind. Above all, they communicate the emotion of what the Japanese call *yugen,* ideal beauty.

The Noh theater can be understood and appreciated more intelligently and more fully when seen in this light and against the background of Japanese art principles and values.

Many scholars, as well as mere visitors to Japan, have written on the Noh. Among the earlier group were Beatrice Lane Suzuki, L. Adams Beck, A. L. Sadler, Arthur Waley, Ernest Fenollosa, Marie C. Stopes, and Joji Sakurai. More recent scholars, both Japanese and

Western, are legion: to name a few—Paul Claudel, Herman Bohner, J. G. Mills, Earle Ernst, Hiro Ishibashi, Henry W. Wells, and Donald Keene. Excellent work has also been done by members of the Japanese Classics Translation Committee, with Sanki Ichikawa as chairman, which was appointed in 1934 by the Nippon Gakujutsu Shinkokai (Japan Society for the Promotion of Science).

Fenollosa was among the first to bring to light the buried treasure of the arts of Japan. Fenollosa, like Pound, was a Harvard man and had gone to Japan in 1878 as a professor of economics at Tokyo Imperial University. Very soon, because of his consuming interest in Oriental art, he was appointed Imperial Commissioner of Fine Arts and eventually became the greatest scholar of his time on China and Japan, promoting, as Pound says, "a new understanding of the East."[10] On his return to the United States in 1890, he became curator of Oriental art at the Boston Museum of Fine Arts. He died in England in 1908, but the Japanese government sent a warship to take his ashes to Japan. His book *Epochs of Japanese and Chinese Art*, published in 1911, is an impressive monument. *'Noh' or Accomplishment* was compiled after Fenollosa's death from his draft of the proposed work on the Noh. Undoubtedly Fenollosa was a great pioneer in introducing Chinese and Japanese art to the West.

Fenollosa was fortunate in coming to know Minoru Umewaka, a survivor of the shogun's Noh troupe after the Meiji Restoration of 1868. He was Fenollosa's teacher and cherished the Noh tradition and kept it from being swept away with the old regime. He sold his own clothes and furniture to buy masks and costumes, possibly heirlooms belonging to a once-wealthy nobility. More than that, he preserved as a holy trust texts of Noh plays, called chantbooks, and the attached acting instructions.

The Japanese theater has two highly traditional forms. The Noh theater originated in a very old folk art that by the end of the fourteenth century had developed into an entertainment suitable to be performed at the shogun's court. The Kabuki, the more modern theater, less than four hundred years old, is the more popular; it features elaborate, colorful settings, a magnificent display of costumes, and a romantic kind of verisimilitude in dialogue and acting. It delights in comedy and melodrama. The Kabuki is gorgeous and spectacular. The Noh is chaste, quiet, and sophisticated.

Fenollosa traces in the history of the Noh three strands of Japanese origin.[11] First there is the sacred dance found in Shinto ritual and characterized by graceful and restrained postures and movements. Like Greek drama and the medieval European miracle play, it has a religious origin. Then with the age of knight-errantry beginning in the thirteenth century, the warrior-aristocrats' dances and music provided a variety of dramatic motifs. Thirdly, Buddhist civilization, based on contemplation and poetic insight, contributed a philosophical outlook and a moral purpose. The priest, the warrior, and finally the player perfected this form of drama as a serious, select art, enacting through symbol and ritual the spiritual experiences of man for the pleasure and contemplation of the cultured class.

Strangely enough, it was at Columbia University in New York, in 1950 while working on Yeats, that I first discovered the Noh theater of Japan. Just before I was to choose the subject for my thesis, Professor W. Y. Tindall, my adviser, asked me: "Have you read the Noh plays?" Frankly puzzled, never having heard of the Noh, I replied: "No, sir, how do you spell it, sir?" The professor, no less frankly puzzled, asked: "Spell what?"

This was the genesis of my master's thesis, "W. B. Yeats's *Four Plays for Dancers*." It started from scratch. At that time very few would have considered such a theme anything short of a leap in the dark. Thereafter, I read with lively excitement all the Noh plays that I could find in English translation, spending much time in the Oriental section of Low Library and other libraries at Columbia. With half the globe between myself and Japan, the Noh seemed something quite out of this world. From all the evidence of Fenollosa, Waley, Claudel, and others I wondered if this exquisite dramatic art was not, in part, made more fabulous by the Western imagination run wild over the Orient. Many years later I had the opportunity to see the Noh in the country of its birth and in the company of Japanese Noh enthusiasts for a whole season and found that it was no myth; that it had vitally existed in the past; that it was vividly alive in modern

Japan, albeit for the relative few; and that its chief appeal for me was precisely its aristocracy and its otherworldliness.

My first experience of the Noh took place on November 4, 1959, at the Suidobashi Nohgakudo theater in Tokyo. The occasion was both memorable and disappointing. The program began at the fashionable evening hour. Tickets were high-priced, and all seats were reserved. The playbill read: "Welcome to Noh drama and Kyogen comedy for foreign tourists and residents under the auspices of the International Noh Drama Club—performed by top-ranking actors according to the orthodox style of the school." There was a hopeful note to say that a full explanation of the performance would be found in English in the playbill and that "actors in costume will sit for pictures after the fall of the curtain." As a last blow to my particular type of expectation, the playbill added: "Cameras are allowed." I was not a little perturbed that it was to be that sort of performance, commercialized in the contemporary manner, entirely out of keeping with the Noh of my reading and imagination.

Though this was to be a modest two-hour performance instead of the usual five to six hours, the tourists and foreign residents kept restlessly moving in and out of the best seats, which my party could not afford. The few Japanese who had come unattended, and the students with whom I had come, remained in solitary splendor, each in his own world, watching and listening while the famous Rokuro Umewaka took the leading role in a favorite play, *Aoi no Ue* (The Lady Aoi), and his son Manzaburo Nomura acted in the Kyogen comedy *Oba-ga-sake* (Aunt's Wine). The two-piece presentation was intended to give a sampling of the Noh. According to my Japanese friends it was a much watered-down version, by no means up to the standard and mood of the traditional drama. Subsequently we were allowed into the sanctum of the greenroom, were introduced to the actors, and held the two-pound Noh masks in our hands.

Even at this first performance, I knew somehow that this Noh had been staged with concessions to the modern audience present rather than with fidelity to the ancient art. What is more, I could fully appreciate the situation. In 1951 Ram Gopal, a famous Indian dancer, and his gifted troupe had given a brilliant and altogether absorbing

exposition of Bharata Natyam in New York, but it had been some-
what spoiled for me by alien touches, such as the quicker tempo of
music, the more pronounced gestures, the stage setting and costumes—all of which were specially oriented toward an American
audience that was probably seeing this Indian classical dance form
for the first time.

No uninitiated audience, however sensitive, could be expected to
take the Noh, a centuries-old and highly specialized art, neat. I had
come for the Noh—neat. So my first personal acquaintance with the
Noh made a mixed, and on the whole a disturbing, impact upon my
sensibility. The real spell came later, when I bought a season ticket for
the classical Noh theater as performed for Japanese connoisseurs at the
Kanze Kaikan in Iidabashi, Tokyo, more than twenty miles from where
I was living, and to the amusement of my Japanese friends saw and enjoyed play after play in complete self-surrender without understanding
a word of Japanese. I was deeply envious of the Japanese Noh-goer, who
had his eyes glued to a much-thumbed script, nobly bound, written in
beautifully brushed calligraply, and who seemed to savor delicately
every phrase as it was chanted or sung by the actors. But oddly
enough, lack of language was no barrier to the poetic experience.
Listening to the classical Karnatic music of South India, especially
the vocal music, even the rudiments of which are beyond my musical
comprehension, I have felt a similar mood of abandonment and an-
imation. The Japanese audience with whom I was witnessing these
plays, I am sure, felt the fascination of the Noh much more. For they
gave the impression of knowing much more than its mere rudiments.
I wonder how much more must the Japanese of the feudal period,
with their love of artistry and their trained sensibility, have seen and
felt in this exquisite drama of music, dream, and reverie.

Forbidden places of popular entertainment and extremely snobbish
in regard to the fine arts, the young noblemen of that time cultivated the more contemplative, stylized, and disciplined forms of the
arts, such as savoring incense (''listening to incense'' in Japanese),
the tea cult, *ikebana,* landscape gardening, and dry-landscape gardens,
all of which have continued to hold a place of honor among sophisti-

cated Japanese, who yet remember, perhaps with nostalgia, the traditional culture of the Land of the Rising Sun. The nobles loved poetry and were well versed in ancient aesthetic norms. They delighted in creating glimpses of truth in experiences of emotional and imaginative states. Withal, they admired, as Reischauer notes, ascetic virtues, physical toughness, mental discipline, and indifference to suffering and death, and prided themselves on family loyalty. The subtle and scrupulously controlled Noh with its insights into unearthly beauty was therefore fully in accord with their Zen outlook, their Spartan character, and their princely tastes.

Noh means "accomplishment," "skill," or "talent." It is said that the term was first applied to actors and dancers. The fourteenth and fifteenth centuries were the golden prime of the Noh, when Kan'ami (1333–84) and his son Zeami (1363–1443) developed this dramatic art and themselves acted with distinction. Zeami's famous treatise *Fushi Kaden*, or *Kadensho* (Book of the Transmission of the Flower), written under the patronage of Yoshimitsu, the third shogun of the Ashikaga family, is the authoritative handbook on the subject. This elaborates the aesthetic principles of the Noh and gives detailed and careful instructions on composition, dance, music, acting, and production in general.

The purpose of the Noh was to teach its courtly audience the concepts of nonattachment and peace, two attitudes outside the vocabulary of the Japanese martial class—hence especially important. In turbulent periods of history, the Noh themes "turned the mind to the Buddha" and presented the emptiness and transitory nature of all earthly splendor, love, heroism, and war. According to Zeami, the most important elements of the Noh, dance and musical chanting, as also the story with supernatural dramatis personae from Japanese myth, legend, and history, were appropriate modes of conveying these philosophical attitudes.

The plot of a Noh play is very slender—a mere fragment with a single sustained mood—and can be best appreciated in relation to the total *bangumi,* or program. In the old days the *bangumi* was protracted over three to five days on ceremonial occasions, such as the initiations and marriages of the shoguns and receptions at the shogun's court of envoys from the imperial court, where the emperor reigned but did not rule. As many as four or five days were assigned to the very central ceremony of the New Year and to rites for the dead shoguns. Sometimes up to ten dramatic pieces were presented between nine in the morning and three in the afternoon. But the usual presentation offered a cycle of life in five plays.

The first play, the *shugen* or *kami No* (god Noh), which is in the nature of a ritualistic religious dance, is in praise of the grandeur and goodness of the gods who protect the land from harm and misfortune. The proud and splendid *shura-mono,* or battle piece, celebrates the deeds of the heroes and warriors of the rival Genji and Heike clans of the twelfth century. Usually the ghost of a warrior of the Genji or Heike clan appears as an ordinary person on the stage, reveals his identity and his tragic tale, then fades away in a dance. In some plays he expels a demon and keeps the peace. Next comes the *onna-mono* (woman piece) or *katsura-mono* (wig piece), so called because female actors are forbidden to appear in the Noh, so male actors wear wigs as well as masks to represent women. The wig or woman piece brings gentleness after the tumult of war scenes and introduces love plots and beautiful women. The most lyrical dances and poetry are to be found in these plays. The repertoire of the fourth group includes a variety of dramatic themes. The play may be a Noh of spirits, such as the exquisite *Aoi no Ue,* in which a woman, obsessed with jealousy, is literally possessed; *Nishikigi,* in which a man and woman whose love was never consummated in life wander disconsolately as ghosts until a Buddhist priest frees them to join in love; or *Motomezuka,* where a young woman suffers agonies in hell. Or, instead of a Noh play, the fourth piece may be a Kyogen, an earthy farce characterized by lively realism, depicting the foibles and weaknesses of mankind. The fifth and last piece, the *kiri No,* has a supernatural protagonist and ends on an auspicious and congratulatory note. It is addressed to the nobles and aristocrats in the audience.

Nowhere in these plays is characterization vigorous. Since the Noh presupposes ancestor worship, it has many supernatural figures, usually ghosts. The difficulty with ghosts is that they evade character portrayal. Therefore characterization as well as bold and strong action are rejected in the Noh in favor of a story of passion or mood represented symbolically.

Originally, performances were given at the shogun's court or at the house of a nobleman, half out-of-doors. The smallness and intimacy of the theater with its conventional shape, every measurement set by Zeami, holds to this day, thanks to the zeal and faithfulness of Minoru Umewaka and his family, who, as was mentioned above, revived the Noh after the Meiji Restoration.

The stage, on a level with the spectators, is a square platform open on three sides. The most striking feature is the twisted, luxuriant pine tree, symbol of permanence in a fleeting scene, painted in vivid green in the center background of the glossy tan wood surface. Bamboo designs are painted on either side of the spreading pine. The same fresh wood lines the walls, the ceiling, and the floor of the stage. The greenroom on the spectators' extreme left is connected with the stage by a long bridgeway or corridor. There is nothing on the right to correspond to the bridgeway. The asymmetry is very pronounced. Three pine saplings in pots, symbols of heaven, earth, and man, placed at intervals along the bridgeway to mark positions of actors in their entrances and exits, are also a reminder that the Noh was originally performed in the open. There is no curtain on the stage. But there is a curtain at the entrance of the long corridor leading from the greenroom to the stage. In sharp contrast to the rest of the unassuming, subdued decor, this is gorgeously colored. It is almost gaudy, with a purple horizontal band at the top to set off the long, flowing, vertical stripes of green, yellow, orange, white, and purple. Orange silk tassels stream on either side of the curtain. At the entrance of the first actor the slow, ceremonious lifting of this curtain creates an atmosphere of hushed expectation in the theater. This is enhanced by the equally slow and meticulously timed steps of the first actor, who glides in with the majesty of a royal procession.

The stage setting is spare. Much is left to the imagination. Nor is there much description of the scene in fine poetry, as is found in the Shakespearean play. An open framework will serve for a boat in a play like *Funa Benkei* (Benkei in the Boat). A hut or palace is easily erected by putting a roof on four bamboo poles. The properties are handed out, when called for, in full view of the audience, with great deftness and dispatch, by the *koken,* or assistant, who is also an understudy for the *shite,* or protagonist. The Japanese fan, capable of representing a diversity of actions and emotions, serves also as a sword, a shield, a dagger.

While the stage is simplicity itself, the costumes are regal and resplendent. The Noh *shozoku,* or costumes, display traditional colors to perfection. The length and cut of the kimono sleeve is precise and plays an important role in acting. One is dazzled by robes of rare beauty, made of rich gold and silver brocade with linings of fine silk. These garments are lovingly preserved by each Noh school for centuries. Noh families pride themselves on their costly heirlooms bought from the old bankrupt troupes. There is an atmosphere of eternity in these old treasures of silk and embroidery.

One of the most distinguished features of the Noh theater is the use of masks. As in ancient Greek drama and in the classical Kathakali dance-drama of South India, masks contribute to the stylized quality of acting and promote and augment the stature and nobility of the characters. They are worn by the *shite,* the *tsure* (his attendant), female and supernatural characters, and old men. Fifteen varieties of masks for different roles, such as those for the hero, the villain, the demon, and the madwoman, specified by the fourteenth- and fifteenth-century masters, still follow traditional usage. They appear again and again on the Noh stage and give the playgoer the complacent pleasure of recognition.

Use of masks dispenses with the necessity for makeup. There are no problems regarding the representation of age or sex or the supernatural. A good actor using a mask made with a neutral expression can give, through a minimum of skillful poses of the head and neck, an unbelievable range of emotional meaning to the masked face. A downward glance turns the expression into one of dejection. An upward glance lights the face with joy and cheer. I never ceased to marvel at this miracle taking place from moment to moment before my very eyes. The narrow slits for the eyes (narrow, half-shut eyes are ideals of Japanese beauty and cause romantic tremors in the beholder, I was told) hold the inner concentration by literally impeding the actor's view of the external world. Cut off from his immediate surroundings, the actor can have a more intense vision of the imaginative role he is called upon to live and act. A Noh mask sometimes weighs two pounds. This weight poised on the head and the difficulty of seeing through narrow slits necessitates slow movement and further compels the subdued quality of acting characteristic of the Noh.

Masks were and still are made by dedicated sculptors. I saw masks of the most exquisite workmanship in the temples of Nara. Every Noh enthusiast spoke glowingly of Nyori Kitazawa of Kyoto, a contemporary maskmaker. He adhered to traditional concepts and took seriously the task of choosing wood of just the right texture, shape, and thickness before carving and painting these highly prized creations. It was said that sometimes he made only two masks a month.

What created in me the most trancelike effect was the music of the Noh. I received the impression that the Japanese Noh-goer was as much under its spell but certainly not because of its novelty, which might partly account for my own state. The habitual Noh-goer often sat with eyes closed, seeming to enjoy the sounds and words more than the spectacle. It has even been averred that the Noh is essentially a musical theater rather than a visual theater. Recordings of Noh music provide for some an experience quite as meaningful as a stage performance. All the subtlety of masked acting, the stylized stage setting, the gorgeousness of costume would be nothing without the strong, almost primitive appeal of the sound of Noh. Nor, paradoxically, is the Noh music itself by any means primitive. It is a highly cultivated art and partakes of the inveterate Japanese habit and ideal of artifice. Perhaps the artifice lies in preserving the spontaneous primitive appeal.

A single man's voice can impersonate many parts. In the case of a solo singer the voice is so completely altered and disguised that not only is there little semblance of the singer's own voice, but little semblance of the human voice. Almost unearthly sounds are produced with the rounded mouth. An interesting quality of the music is the impression of a dialogue between sound and echo. One finds a similar device in the classical Karnatic music of South India, where the voice is echoed by an instrument or one instrument is echoed by another. In the Noh music two people alternate this sound, and the echo effect is duplicated in the words. For instance, in the Noh play *Uto* by Zeami the call of the parent *uto* (a bird of northern Japan similar to a snipe or wild duck) is "ootow" and that of its young is "yass-kata," both doubtless in the nature of onomatopoeia. The flavor of the original composition can be sensed in the English translation of the play, where in imitation of the bird's call half the line is repeated as an echo. Below are three examples:

Then, penitent, he descends to the foot of the mountain . . . to the foot of the mountain, penitent . . .

Gives it with tears to the wandering monk . . . with tears, to the wandering monk. . . .

And then vanishes, no one knows where . . . no one knows where. . . .[12]

Especially intriguing for me was the solo singer, who produced guttural sounds of *g* and *gh* akin to those in Arabic and Urdu and which reminded me of the *aazan*, the Muslim call to prayer, or the chanting of the Quran. I have never felt such a nostalgia for my upbringing in Indian Islamic traditions as I did on hearing Japanese vocal music far from my homeland.

The Noh orchestra consists of a shoulder drum, a knee drum—one high-pitched, one low and soft—and possibly an additional flat drum; a flute capable of shrill, lonely piping; and an eight-man chorus rhythmically chanting words. All of these continuously provide a blended musical background. A double set of boards at the back of the stage and five earthenware jars placed at mathematically determined distances under the stage enrich the tone of the music and produce unexpected echoes and reverberations.

Arranged in their conventional, asymmetrical manner in front of the painted pine, the musicians are seated in readiness for the *shite* to appear. The chorus sits at the side of the stage directly opposite the bridgeway. The musical exposition is always slow and deliberate —first there is one still, bewitching monologue chanted to the insistent beat of the drums. The songs and lyrics, mere threads of the poetry of suggestion, sung in a plaintive wistful way, each syllable carefully pronounced and each stop consciously made at regular intervals, have a haunting quality and leave a feeling of evanescence and regret. The rest of the music proceeds in enchanting and progressively more complex rhythms until it builds up the full emotional tone. As observed in *The Noh Drama,* the flutist, who had earlier quietened the audience and indicated the nature of the play, now carries the whole production to "a climax of dramatic ecstasy."[13]

Noh acting and dancing are looked upon as God-given vocations and are passed on from generation to generation with hereditary pride. The long genealogy of the Umewaka family is complicated and impressive. It is claimed that Minoru Umewaka was the forty-fifth-generation descendant of this ancient line.[14] A good Noh actor is expected not only to achieve the necessary mastery of his art but also to create the feeling and sympathy that enable both him and the audience to know that the actor himself is the god, the madwoman, the old man. No female actors are allowed on the Noh stage, nor for that matter on the Kabuki stage, and among the most celebrated actors are those who can act female parts well. A story is told repeatedly in literature on the Noh of an actor who followed an old woman to study her gait and was rebuked and told to find it in his heart. A lifetime training as rigorous as that of Plato's philosopher-king, Noh acting demands from the age of five to the age of forty-five a constant discipline in gesture and action, as well as in imagination and feeling, to make it effective.

Instead of generalizing on Noh acting, I have expanded, below, jottings I made at one of the dozen Noh performances I saw at the Kanze Kaikan in Tokyo. I have picked out features from the several plays that were performed that day.

There was not only silence in the playhouse, but a solemn, hushed atmosphere like that of a church service and fraught with expectation. The eight singers, the drummers, and the flutist took their own time to arrange themselves upstage, leaving the rest of the space vacant for acting and dancing. The groupings on the stage were meticulously asymmetrical.

In one play, *Saigyo-zakura,* a green circular tent, with foliage and blossoms stuck on top representing a cherry tree, was brought in ceremoniously and placed at the right of the stage. The music began slowly, and a priest in a seated position raised aloft his rosary, held in both hands. Then all eyes turned in the direction of the entrance to the long bridgeway on the extreme left, where the lifting of the flamboyant curtain on two invisible bamboo poles provided a ceremony in itself. The *shite,* looking to neither right nor left, with the upper part of his body well poised and arms and hands close to his sides, appeared like a ghost gliding in ritualistic movements, slowly planting first the heels on the wooden floor and bringing the toes to rest last of all. It took an eternity for him to cover the distance marked by the three pines and reach his appointed position on the stage. The *shite* moved like a ghost, but in appearance he was very unlike one. He was dressed as a nobleman in white lower garments and white *tabi* (split-toed socks), with blue and gold upper garments and with dashes of red and brown cord very pleasing to the eye. He carried a fan and was followed by a symbolic retinue of courtiers carrying swords. The courtiers were in formal dress. The most fantastic feature of the courtiers' dress was the lower part, which not only covered legs and feet but trailed behind in double measure, flapping like the tails of mermaids. Japanese medieval court etiquette prescribed that no part of the human anatomy except the face was to be exposed in the presence of superiors.

In the role of the ghost in one play the actor appeared with a kimono held tentwise over his head, as did the spirit of the cherry tree in *Saigyo-zakura.* Sometimes two scenes were enacted simultaneously by two sets of actors, each oblivious of the other. Travel was represented by the actor crossing the stage hat in hand. On his exit the actor abruptly turned his back to the audience and stamped his feet emphatically twice before departing.

Each actor was allowed a good share of the time to perform his solo part and held a single pose for minutes together, with pauses long enough to make a modern audience fall out of patience. One had to wait for even the breathing to indicate some emotional nuance. The acting and dancing, to the accompaniment of solo or group chanting, with the strong beat of the drum and the shrill, delicate piping of the flute, continued as the masked face turned in stylized poses to express and expand the drift of the economical, concentrated text.

The spirit of the cherry tree in *Saigyo-zakura* danced for a full half-hour in utterly enraptured mood while the other actors sat still on the stage. The dance with its slow rhythmic steps, the movements of the flowing kimono sleeves, and the measured gestures of the fan was choreographed with artistic subtlety (which nevertheless seemed simple to the layman) until the whole gained in momentum and came to a climax in delicately controlled ecstasy. In the absence of a curtain and with no change of scene, the transitions from one action to another merged in an uninterrupted flow.

I was struck by the magnificent representation of the slow and insidious conquest by insanity in the play *Aoi no Ue*, in which the Lady Rokujo, inflamed with jealousy because Prince Genji, her former lover, had drifted to the Lady Aoi, suffers the burning torments of loss and regret. The neutral mask, with the almost imperceptible movement of the eyes seen through the slits, recorded marvelously the demoniac and forlorn condition of her agonized spirit. One sleeve falling over her shoulder and hanging disconsolately down her side, a conventional indication of a state of distraction (for the Noh actor there is only one correct way of doing things), the woman searched her fan, holding it away from herself, as if it—the fan—were her last refuge and contained the text of her whole predicament and of her fate. Locked in a private, closed world of anguish and loneliness, the madwoman danced in hypnotized abandon, creating most movingly the forsaken state of the sick mind. It was a spell not easy to break. But broken it was, for when his part was over, the dancer stopped abruptly, turned his back to the audience, stamped his feet twice, and all the magic, the make-believe, and the absorption on the part of the beholder faded in a trice and he came back to himself with a rude jolt. In other plays the acting and dancing exhibited superb displays of other emotions—secret joy, envy, turmoil, triumph, bliss, serenity. The Noh is a theater that makes one feel. In that it is extremely lyrical and subjective.

It is a matter for regret that Yeats had no opportunity to see the Noh staged in the land of its birth. His knowledge of the Noh came to him through Pound, Fenollosa, and others. This was clearly a theater after his own heart. It had aristocracy, poetry, ritual, the ghost world, the rapt dance, liturgical music, myth, and symbolism—in short, all those elements that conspire to produce a visionary world through the witchery of stylized, lyrical drama.

Yeats's response was immediate, and his approach to the new theater was all his own. In 1921 a volume of new plays called *Four Plays for Dancers* was published; it contained *At the Hawk's Well, The Only Jealousy of Emer, The Dreaming of the Bones,* and *Calvary.*

Four   YEATS AND THE
                                PLAYS FOR DANCERS

Accomplished fingers begin to play . . .

THE UNDIVIDED ATTENTION given to the Noh theater of Japan in the last chapter was intentional. Now it is not difficult to see why Ezra Pound said: "It is a stage of which Mr. Yeats may approve," and why Yeats wrote: "My blunder has been that I did not discover in my youth that my theatre must be the ancient theatre that can be made by unrolling a carpet or marking out a place with a stick or setting a screen against the wall. . . . I have found my first model . . . in the Noh stage of aristocratic Japan."[1]

Nor was it, I think, merely a matter of the portable carpet, in other words, of stagecraft. Yeats felt that the Noh play would also help "to explain a certain possibility of the Irish dramatic movement"[2] and Irish national aspirations. So he proceeded to find parallels between Irish legend and stories of Shinto gods, ghosts, and warriors. The popular Noh play *Nishikigi* recalled to his mind Lady Gregory's story of the Aran boy and the lovers who sought forgiveness for bartering away their country. The dramatic themes of most of his new plays for dancers were centered in Irish history and myth, but for dramatic technique Yeats drew heavily on the Noh. In this chap-

59

ter I intend to discuss chiefly the dramatic technique he created after the manner of the Noh theater.

It is well to remember that Yeats was not attempting some happy blend of the East and the West, so favored in our twentieth-century civilization. He was too much of a universalist not to see the beauty and significance of diversity. Nor was he creating anything like a replica of the Noh. He was looking for art forms that would appeal to his sophisticated, fastidious taste whether the art form came from Europe or Japan. In the preface to *The Cutting of an Agate* Yeats writes: "I was busy with a single art, that of a small unpopular theatre: and this art may well seem to practical men busy with some programme of industrial or political regeneration . . . of no more account than the shaping of an agate; and yet in the shaping of an agate, whether in the cutting or in the making of the design, one discovers, if one have a speculative mind, thoughts that seem important and principles that may be applied to life itself."[3] The writing and the producing of *At the Hawk's Well,* the first of the plays for dancers, must surely have been the cutting and shaping of a precious stone. The substitution of Irish subjects for Japanese ones was probably the only easy thing for a mind amply stocked with tales of old Ireland, especially those of the heroic age—of Finn and Cuchulain and Usnach's children. The rest was sore labor, chiseling the material chosen and molding it to an art form at once subtle, stylized, and alien.

The intentions of Yeats might be better illustrated if one or two of the Japanese plays are briefly analyzed at this juncture to see what elements of the Noh were absorbed into *Four Plays for Dancers.* Of the many Noh plays I have read and seen, *Hagoromo, Nishikigi, Dojoji,* and *Aoi no Ue* are among the most beautiful and engaging. Yeats read the first two in the translations by Fenollosa and Pound and published in *Certain Noble Plays of Japan.* In *Hagoromo* (The Feather Mantle), Hakuryo, a fisherman, finding by good luck a beautiful cloak in the pine grove at Mio Bay, where he is accustomed to fish, is about to take it home when a celestial maiden appears and claims it for her own. The covetous Hakuryo refuses to part with it. But when the maiden pleads with him to give it back (for otherwise she would be shut out of her sky-home), he returns it on the promise of a dance. So much for the simple plot.

Hagoromo is played on a bare stage in the traditional way with a small chorus, a flute, and three drums. The chorus and a fisherman are describing the landscape, the scene of action, when Hakuryo arrives with the robe of feathers and announces who he is and what he has found. A masked maiden described as sumptuously dressed in satin with peacock feathers in brilliant colors, a high gold crown, velvet shoes, and a fan appears forthwith and a dialogue boding a crisis, a quarrel at least on the fisherman's side, takes place, until the identity and plight of the maiden are revealed. Whereupon the tone changes magically and the fisherman forgoes his lately acquired wealth in exchange for a dance. The imagery has reference to feathery things, such as the "plumage of heaven" and the "feathery skirt of the stars," which Yeats noted with delight. The final dance, which is the maiden's ascent to heaven, depicting the changes and beauties of the moon in its round of nights, and the intoning of the chorus create a single mood of joy mingled with wistfulness at the fleeting, precious glimpses of beauty vouchsafed to man in the midst of his mundane tasks and at the sad mutability of all earth's fairest things. "Fuji is gone; the great peak of Fuji is blotted out little by little. It melts into the upper mist. In this way she . . . is lost to sight."[4]

But the play that had a direct and strong influence on Yeats was *Nishikigi*. The resemblance between this and Yeats's *Dreaming of the Bones* is striking and can be seen in the theme, story, structure, and spirit of the two plays. The theme in both is conscience troubled by guilt and remorse and the inability of the protagonists to escape their past—a favorite motif in the Noh. In both plays the plot is simple and slender. In *Nishikigi,* the ghosts of two lovers who had not married each other in life return after death to haunt the scene of their unhappy lives until they meet a priest, tell him their agonized tale, and plead with him to perform the wedding rites. Thereafter their spirits no longer wander disconsolate and homeless upon the earth. As is customary in the Noh, the identity of the lovers is disclosed during the course of their meeting with the priest. Also, it is always denizens of the other world that relate their tragic plight, while the listener is someone from this earthly life. In another Noh play, *Motomezuka,* a maiden tells the priest about her rejected lover's suicide and seeks expiation for her share in the crime.

In his 1914 essay "Swedenborg, Mediums, Desolate Places," Yeats writes: "All spirits [that] for some time after death . . . cannot become disengaged from old habits and desires . . . it may be for centuries keep the shapes of these earthly bodies and carry on their old activities, wooing or quarrelling . . . in a round of dull duties or passionate events."[5] This belief, the plot of *Nishikigi,* and the national, patriotic theme together formed an attractive basis for Yeats's play *The Dreaming of the Bones* (1917). It is a ghost play, and its story comes from Irish legend. The souls of Diarmuid and Dervorgilla, who had been lovers in free ancient Ireland and who had betrayed their country into the hands of the conquering Normans, do penance for centuries to expiate this political crime against their people. Troubled by the memory of a treacherous deed, they dream back and haunt the scenes of their earthly life in the hope of finding a fellow countryman to absolve them and to give peace to their wandering souls. As far as the subject goes, the paralled between *Nishikigi* and *The Dreaming of the Bones* ends here. Whereas *Nishikigi* evokes the past and presents a human situation that is universal, *The Dreaming of the Bones* presents a human situation that is universal, but evokes the past not for its own sake but to interpret a contemporary event—the 1916 political uprising in Ireland, which was ruthlessly put down by the British. The play, as in the Noh, opens with a lyric of foreboding. The following lines are sung by the musicians while the folding and unfolding of the cloth (not a Noh feature) takes place:

> Why does my heart beat so?
> Did not a shadow pass?
> . . . .
> Have not old writers said
> That dizzy dreams can spring
> From the dry bones of the dead?
> And many a night it seems

That all the valley fills
With those fantastic dreams.
They overflow the hills,
So passionate is a shade,
Like wine that fills to the top
A grey-green cup of jade,
Or maybe an agate cup.

The first musician then describes the landscape, and while the birds are crying in their loneliness a rebel hunted by the British army, waiting to be rescued by his party, encounters a stranger and a young girl on a barren rocky hill. To show that the ghostly couple and the rebel fisherman are separated from each other by seven centuries, the former wear masks. The Aran fisherman is the contemporary to whom the thus far unidentified lovers tell their tormented story. Like the priest in *Nishikigi,* he is the listener. But the moment the names of the lovers and their guilt are disclosed, the young man's attitude changes precipitously from sympathy to utter condemnation:

YOUNG MAN.   You speak of Diarmuid and Dervorgilla
  Who brought the Norman in?
YOUNG GIRL.   Yes, yes, I spoke
  Of that most miserable, most accursed pair
  Who sold their country into slavery; and yet
  They were not wholly miserable and accursed
  If somebody of their race at last would say,
  'I have forgiven them'.
YOUNG MAN.   O, never, never
  Shall Diarmuid and Dervorgilla be forgiven.

He repeats the emphatic "never, never" line and acknowledges that he was taken in by their story, so movingly told by the girl; but now he rejects the lovers coldly and utterly, and proceeds to go about his own business: ". . . better push on now. / The horizon to the east is growing bright." The realism of these lines shatters the illusion under which the lovers had been living, or rather dreaming. In the Noh the ghost who is dreaming back always finds a priest to absolve him or her. In *The Dreaming of the Bones* the Aran fisherman is rigid, unfeeling, and patriotic. His rejection of the lovers is conveyed in his sad and angry thoughts as from the summit of the hill he reviews Irish history and the late destruction caused by the English troopers in the Aran islands, Connemara hills, and Galway:

> . . . That town had lain,
> But for the pair that you would have me pardon,
> Amid its gables and its battlements
> Like any old admired Italian town;
> . . . .
> Our country, if that crime were uncommitted,
> Had been most beautiful.

The play closes in a mood of dejection and despair as the lovers retreat to the ghost world in a tormented dance. "Being folded up and hidden in their dance" the lovers drift away "from rock to rock" "as though their hearts / Had suddenly been broken." The Aran youth is relieved to have weathered the temptation. "I had almost yielded and forgiven it all— / Terrible the temptation and the place!" And he hastens away, for he is really bent on his own escape both physical and spiritual. The Irish rebellion of 1916 is poignantly presented through the symbolism of the two guilt-ridden lovers of the past. As does *Nishikigi, The Dreaming of the Bones* ends in a dance and exquisite lyrics. The red cock and "March birds a-crow" stand for betrayal and by reference to Peter's denial of Christ heighten the tragedy of Diarmuid and Dervorgilla:

> What finger first began
> Music of a lost kingdom?
> They dream that laughed in the sun.
> Dry bones that dream are bitter,
> They dream and darken our sun.
> . . . .
> My heart ran wild when it heard
> The curlew cry before dawn
> And the eddying cat-headed bird;

But now the night is gone.
I have heard from far below
The strong March birds a-crow.
Stretch neck and clap the wing,
Red cocks, and crow!

Turning to *Four Plays for Dancers* in general, on technical matters we find every possible simplification of stage setting. Minute and careful instructions for production are given by Yeats in the preface to *Four Plays for Dancers* and in separate notes on each play, together with stage directions in the text of each.

All four plays are intended to be performed in a drawing room or studio, with the audience surrounding a stage stripped of all properties except the most indispensable ones, such as a bed for Cuchulain's body in *The Only Jealousy of Emer* and the cross in *Calvary*. A curtain or screen is set against the back wall, decorated with a design suggesting a hawk in *At the Hawk's Well* or a mountain against the sky in *The Dreaming of the Bones*. Yeats wanted "half a dozen players who can bring all the properties in a cab and perform in their leisure moments."[6]

As a substitute for the rising of the curtain each play opens and closes with the unfolding and folding of the cloth. For instance, in *At the Hawk's Well* the first musician goes to the center with a folded black cloth hanging from his fingers and stands motionless. Then a musician enters from each side of the stage; they pause a moment and proceed to the center to unfold the cloth. The chorus in each play consists of the three musicians, who either in unison or in turn open the play with songs of great lyric beauty to indicate the nature and mood of the play. It is specified in the notes for the production of these plays that instruments on Oriental lines, such as the drum, zither, flute, and a gong with a mellow sound, are to be used. The gong in particular, Yeats felt, deepened the emotional tone of the play. The chanting of verse, the singing by the chorus, and the dances are all accompanied by these instruments.

Except for *Calvary*, the musical score, written either by Walter Rummel or Edmund Dulac, is attached to the script. The musicians also describe the landscape. At the end of each play there is a song to gather up the emotional atmosphere and meaning of the piece, as we have seen in the case of *The Dreaming of the Bones*. As in the Noh, the cast of the play is very small. Excluding the three musicians, *Calvary* has the largest number of characters—six; *The Only Jealousy of Emer* has five, and *At the Hawk's Well* and *The Dreaming of the Bones* have only three each. That Yeats recognized the noncommercial nature of the plays for dancers is revealed in his comment: "Where can I find Mr. Dulac and Mr. Rummel or any to match them but in London or Paris, and who but the leisured will welcome an elaborate art or pay for its experiment."[7]

Yeats was so enamored of the idea of masked players that he fell into extravagance. Every single character in these four plays except the rebel in *The Dreaming of the Bones,* who belongs to contemporary Ireland, is fitted with a mask or is instructed to have his face made up to resemble a mask. Even the musicians are given masks. In the Noh play, as we said in the last chapter, only certain roles are assigned masks. There must have been a great dearth of good masks, for only those designed by sculptors, such as Edmund Dulac and the Dutch sculptor Hildo van Krop, were acceptable to Yeats. Van Krop made masks for *The Only Jealousy of Emer* when this play was staged in Holland.

"If I write plays and organise performances," wrote Yeats in the preface to *Four Plays for Dancers,* "on any scale and with any system, I shall hope for a small number of typical masks, each capable of use in several plays. The face of the speaker should be as much a work of art as the lines that he speaks . . . that all may be as artificial as possible. Perhaps in the end one would write plays for certain masks."[8] Why not? Yeats wished some fine sculptor would make masks for Christ, Lazarus, and Judas for his *Calvary.* He acknowledged again and again his debt to Edmund Dulac for fashioning interesting masks for his plays. Edmund Dulac was a talented artist and skillful mask maker. He made masks for other occasions also. Yeats wrote that none of "these plays could have existed if Edmund Dulac had not taught me the value and beauty of the mask and rediscovered how to design and make it."[9]

Yeats was thrilled with the idea of substituting a mask "for the face of some commonplace player, or for that face repainted to suit his own vulgar fancy."[10] Again, "what could be more suitable than that Cuchulain, let us say, a half-supernatural legendary person, should show to us a face not made before a looking-glass . . . but modelled by some distinguished artist? . . . Nor has anyone told me after a performance that they have missed a changing facial expression, for the mask seems to change with the light that falls upon it, and besides in poetical and tragic art . . . expression is mainly in those movements that are of the entire body."[11] Also, the strangeness and formality of masked players moving "a little stiffly and gravely like marionettes"[12] contributed richly to the ritualistic atmosphere that Yeats so ardently desired.

Costumes were arranged with equal fastidiousness. The versatile Dulac was responsible for designing the costume worn by the guardian of the well in *At the Hawk's Well*. It is an impressive costume as shown in the frontispiece of the 1921 Macmillan edition of *Four Plays for Dancers*. The powerful wings brood ominously over the whole play. In *The Dreaming of the Bones* the lovers are instructed to wear costumes of old times. On the other hand, Cuchulain's grave-clothes must have been simple enough.

The dancing was also to be stylized—"a smaller gamut of expression, something more reserved, and more self-controlled as befits performers within arm's reach of their audience."[13] Only a dancer like Michio Ito, who played the guardian of the well in the first performances of *At the Hawk's Well*, could have danced with slow gliding, graceful movements, formal gestures, and intervals of stillness in the authentic Noh style.

A stage technique of this nature, closely parallel to that of the Noh in all details, could keep a poetic play from the intrusion of the "pushing world" that Yeats wanted to escape in order that a "group of figures, images, and symbols [would] enable us to pass for a few moments into a deep of the mind that had hitherto been too subtle for our habitation."[14]

The presentation of the subject in a one-act play through a simple plot and symbol, as in the Noh, further encouraged this ideal. As in the Noh, the plot of each play is a single action. Outwardly, little happens. The imagery is consistently repeated to charge it with the burden of the principal mood or passion. For example, the songs in *Calvary* are full of herons, hawks, eagles, swans. These birds are symbols of subjectivity. In the notes to *Calvary* Yeats writes: "I have used my bird-symbolism . . . to increase the objective loneliness of Christ, by contrasting it with a loneliness, opposite in kind, that unlike his, can be, whether joyous or sorrowful, sufficient to itself. I have surrounded Him with the images of those He cannot save. . . . the birds, who have served neither God nor Caesar and await for none or for a different saviour."[15] The following dialogue from *Calvary* will show what is meant here:

THIRD MUSICIAN.

    The ger-eagle has chosen his part
    In blue deep of the upper air
    Where one-eyed day can meet his stare;
    He is content with his savage heart.

SECOND MUSICIAN.

    God has not appeared to the birds.

FIRST MUSICIAN.

    But where have last year's cygnets gone?
    The lake is empty; why do they fling
    White wing out beside white wing?
    What can a swan need but a swan?

SECOND MUSICIAN.

    God has not appeared to the birds.

"The shaping of an agate" indeed resulted in a choice, classical art. Nor are *Four Plays for Dancers* the only plays written in this style. *The Cat and the Moon* (1926), *The Resurrection* (1931), *A Full Moon in March* (1935), and *The Death of Cuchulain* (1939) are all dance plays. *Fighting the Waves* is a prose version of *The Only Jealousy of Emer* and shows Yeats's preoccupation with this form as late as 1929, ten years after the verse version was written, in spite of the difficulty of producing it on the stage. Finally, all the plays have a quality of trance, such as the Irish bards are said to have fallen into for nine days at a time and such as a classical Noh production induces in the audience even today. All the plays for dancers are marked by a rare poetic vision, grace, and subtlety. They demonstrate Yeats's theory of distance and intimacy in the theater, and their atmosphere and total effect are unique in the history of Western drama.

Five

THE SPLENDOR AND SORROWS OF THE RED BRANCH: ABOUT "AT THE HAWK'S WELL" AND "THE ONLY JEALOUSY OF EMER"

And all complexities of fury leave . . .

IN THE LAST CHAPTER WE SAW BRIEFLY, with illustrations mainly from *The Dreaming of the Bones,* how Yeats appropriated some of the technical aspects of the Noh theater. There is yet another angle from which Yeats approached that theater. This has to do with his treatment of his subject matter, which except for *Calvary* in *Four Plays for Dancers* he took from traditional Irish stories and legends. I would like to concentrate on the Cuchulain legend in *At the Hawk's Well* and *The Only Jealousy of Emer* and examine how this half-supernatural, half-heroic subject was eminently suited not only to the Noh dramatic technique but, more particularly, to a symbolic rather than a realistic treatment of human situations and human passions.

Long before Yeats came to know the Noh drama he had tended toward a symbolic vision of the subjects of his poetry. He had felt all along that symbols were perhaps the only means of portraying complicated states of mind and experiences in which irony, paradox, and contradiction played a large part. His search for new and significant symbols had led him to explore a diversified field, including Neoplatonism, the Kabbala, Theosophy, Oriental mysticism, the works of William Blake, and contemporary European symbolists. Hence it is not so much that he discovered in the Noh the use of symbolism as a strong feature of the poetic style as that he found therein a vindication of his own theories and of his own partiality for this literary method. In his later poetry and in many of his plays, whether they are written in the Noh manner or in the Western manner, he used symbols with superb mastery to create the kind of experience that defies literal treatment, that offers no cut-and-dried solution but often forces one into positions of irresolution and uncertainty.

Yeats's preoccupation with Ireland is seen in longish poems like "The Wanderings of Oisin" (1889), "The Old Age of Queen Maeve" (1903), and "Baile and Aillinn" (1903), along with several short lyrics of the same period, notably "Cuchulain's Fight with the Sea." But since his desire was for dramatic form, he wrote many plays based on legends from the heroic age of Ireland, which had been arranged and rendered into English by Lady Gregory in *Cuchulain of Muirthemne*. Yeats's praise of this alluring and epochal volume is generous. In his preface to the book he writes: " . . . it is the best book that has ever come out of Ireland; for the stories which it tells are a chief part of Ireland's gift to the imagination of the world."[1]

Except for *Deirdre* (1907) and *The Dreaming of the Bones,* all the plays of Yeats based on the stories of the Red Branch of Ulster are about Cuchulain. There emerges in the end a cycle of the life and death of a splendid and exciting figure of ancient Irish legend to enrich dramatic literature. If taken not in the order in which they were written and published but in the order of events in Cuchulain's life, the saga consists of the following plays:

At the Hawk's Well (published 1917)
The Green Helmet (1910)
On Baile's Strand (1904)
The Only Jealousy of Emer (1919)
Fighting the Waves (1929; a prose version of *Emer*)
The Death of Cuchulain (1939)

"I swear by the oath of my people," said Cuchulain, "I will make my doings be spoken of among the great doings of heroes in their strength."[2] The central character in these plays is Cuchulain, celebrated hero of the Red Branch in the first century A.D., "Cuchulain mysterious to men and beloved of women.'' This reckless, intense, turbulent personality whose name is surrounded by nobility, battle, and fame engaged Yeats's attention for over twenty years. *On Baile's Strand,* the first play on the subject, was written in 1904 and the last, *The Death of Cuchulain,* in 1938, the year before the poet's own death. Why was Cuchulain such a persistent theme in the midst of Yeats's many other preoccupations? There are several reasons.

In her dedication of *Cuchulain of Muirthemne* to the people of Kiltartan, Lady Augusta Gregory writes: "For although you have not to go far to get stories of Finn and Goll and Oisin from any old person in the place, there is very little of the history of Cuchulain . . . left in the memory of the people."[3] It is interesting to note that a statue was raised to Cuchulain in the Dublin Post Office as a monument to the 1916 rebels. Cuchulain must remain "in the memory of the people." This may have been Yeats's motivation, too. What Douglas Hyde, J. M. Synge, and Father Dineen were doing for folklore and fairy tales in Gaelic or folk idiom, Yeats wanted to do for the heroic age in verse. The noble past roused his imagination. It spoke to him of things learned from Lady Gregory, "knowledge of that top of the world where men and women are valued for their manhood and their charm, not for their opinions."[4]

His own family background contained memories of proud, eccentric ancestors. His grandfather William Butler Yeats, rector of Tullylish in County Down, "risked his life to visit and comfort the dying" during a cholera epidemic. John Butler Yeats, Yeats's father, was contemptuous of worldly success, of "getting on in the world," and believed in "poetic and artistic institutions." On his mother's side, the Pollexfens owned ships and roved the seas. They were "silent, instinctive and deep-feeling," and rather unconventional and ceremonious in their way of life.[5] In "Reveries over Childhood and Youth" Yeats reminisces about his grandfather William Pollexfen, who "had won the freedom of some Spanish city, for saving life perhaps, but was so silent that his wife never knew it till he was near eighty."[6] Yeats's father read him exciting stories like Macaulay's *Lays of Ancient Rome,* Sir Walter Scott's *Lay of the Last Minstrel,* and the *Iliad.* He took the boy at the age of ten or twelve to see Henry Irving play Hamlet, who became for Yeats "the image of heroic self-possession." The young Yeats found himself "walking with an artificial stride in memory of Hamlet."[7] Having lived among the landed gentry of Sligo, which retained some of the flavor of feudal times, Yeats conceived a great attraction for the aristocratic personages of his childhood both in life and in fiction.

Cecil Day Lewis emphasizes the importance of this aristocratic tradition in determining Yeats's attitudes and manner of writing. Whatever was excellent in a given culture Yeats attributed to the peasant, the poet, and the aristocrat. They were, for him, the "creative minority" of Toynbee. And it cannot be denied that, for instance, the learning and the great cathedrals of the Middle Ages were sponsored by kings and clerics, the creative minority of a feudal civilization. In modern times the "creative minority" is no longer an elite minority. The credit for whatever a technological civilization produces must go to the prosperous mass of the middle class. Nevertheless, Yeats mistrusted the middle class, feeling that it lacked ceremony, courtesy, and individuality.

Apart from his deep affinity with the aristocratic way of life, in choosing Cuchulain for his subject Yeats shows another side of himself. He loved energetic character. He states with pride that his grandfather William Pollexfen was a man of physical prowess and had "the reputation of never ordering a man to do anything he would not do himself."[8] But there was more here than admiration for mere physical strength. He confesses: "Even today when I read *King Lear* his [William Pollexfen's] image is always before me and I often wonder if the delight in passionate men in my plays and in my poetry is more than his memory."[9] Yeats delighted in action, in the stir of battle, in conflict, not only in the world outside but within oneself. The theory of the mask, which took full shape in *A Vision,* was fundamentally an exploration of strife between the self and the antiself. Cuchulain was for Yeats a symbol of the brisk, passionate, complicated personality.

The most obvious reason for fixing upon the epic age of Ireland as a poetic theme is the factor already discussed in the last chapter, that is, to see how the stylized technique of the Noh plays of Japan gains one distance from the world of day-to-day affairs. Additional distance is achieved through remoteness of subject matter. The remote subject, however, is not used for its own sake. It can interpret contemporary events and universal human situations by awakening "ancient memories," as was seen in *The Dreaming of the Bones*.

Yeats's return to the past does not partake of the nostalgia found in many poets and novelists of the nineteenth century. His work manifests little of the backward-looking spirit of Tennyson's lines "Or that the past will always bring / A glory from its being far." The mood created by Yeats's plays of the heroic age of Ireland cannot be compared with that found in any other revival of antiquity of which I know, beginning with Malory's narrative of the Arthurian legend. Sir Walter Scott's novels re-create the pageantry, glamor, and clash of medieval chivalry. Keats's imagination is wistfully moved by the beauty and eternity of Hellenic art and medieval stories. Later, Tennyson's *Idylls of the King* produces a false picture of King Arthur and the Round Table, seen characteristically in terms of the manners, morals, thoughts, and feelings of Victorian society. William Morris's *Earthly Paradise* of "golden Greece" and of "dim mediaeval times" expresses still another kind of nostalgia for the archaic.

The difference in the poetic attitudes to history and legend of Yeats and these writers does not necessarily lie in the superior worth of one over another. The distinction is one of kind. In Yeats's idea of the past, the time factor is absent, or rather, it is irrelevant. This can best be illustrated by reference to his belief in Anima Mundi, the Great Memory of Nature, which is timeless in the Platonic sense. In Anima Mundi, memories of events, personages, profound states of the soul, dream, and prophecy are stored eternally, regardless of the passing centuries. Here a mingling of minds is possible and "all passionate moments recur again and again."[10] Cuchulain is a symbol of vehement, impassioned experiences in love and war. Diarmuid and Dervorgilla are symbols of guilt and remorse. One is not reminded that these figures lived in some lost legendary time. In *The Dreaming of the Bones* one does not receive the impression that the twentieth-century Aran fisherman is separated by seven centuries from the lovers of legend. Time, in Yeats's work, has an inner consecutivity, if such a term is permitted. It is not measured by the natural round of the seasons or tabulated by calendar dates. It is Byzantium—out of the flux of externally measured time. This feeling one has of the multiplicity of time in some of Yeats's work does not mean that historical time has no meaning for him. As an intellectual concept time is valid and indispensable, but in emotional states it makes little difference. What does it matter that it happened to people in remote ages or that it happens to us today, whatever it is that happens? Yeats sums up: "Every incident in the old rut of birth, love, pain, death has cropped up unchanged for centuries."[11]

Lady Gregory begins the story of Cuchulain in the old-fashioned way: "In the time long ago, Conchubar, Son of Ness, was King of Ulster, and he held his court in the palace of Emain Macha."[12] Here was a grand legendary world of half-supernatural beings, illustrious heroes, women of indescribable beauty: a world of romance and fable, yet curiously tinged with a realism that took account of quilts, coverings, beds, pillows, meat and drink. Conchubar, High King of the Red Branch of Ulster, gained his crown through the craftiness of his mother, who outwitted the dreamy Fergus with her practical wisdom. Conchubar was "wise in his judgments, and brave in battle, and good in shape and form."[13] He was well liked and was surrounded by twelve chief heroes, the flower of the court at Emain Macha, among whom were Conall the Victorious, Laegaire the Battle Winner, Fergus the Visionary, and the three high-born sons of Usnach; and of course Cuchulain, the Hound of Culain, the bravest of the brave, the hero with "seven lights in his eyes,"[14] of whom Emer, his wife, boasts: "And my husband is Cuchulain. . . . There is blood on his spear, . . . his white body is black with blood, his soft skin is furrowed with sword cuts, there are many wounds on his thigh . . . he is the strong protector; . . . he leaps in the air like a salmon when he makes his hero leap; he does strange feats."[15] None could compare with him in courage, magnanimity, honor, virtue. His name was a song on the lips of the people.

Emain Macha had its court poet, too. Sencha, son of Aileel, "chief judge and chief poet of Ulster," was "good in disputes . . . not forgetful . . . [arbiter] between quarrels of kings." He was a skillful orator, able to move assemblies and raise armies; in short, for all his visionary and contemplative qualities he was a man of action among men of the world. Emain Macha also had its devils. Morrigu, goddess of war, was feared and dreaded. Bricriu of the Bitter Tongue, maker of discord, spent a whole year preparing a feast for Conchubar with the sole purpose of fanning strife among the chiefs. He caused a war of words among the fair women of Ulster. It seemed not at all incongruous for Emer of the Yellow Hair and Fedelm of the Fresh Heart to wrangle like peasant women and call each other cows until Sencha the poet rebuked them: "Have done with this word-fighting. . . . It is through the fault of women the shields of men are broken. . . . Wives of heroes, keep yourselves from this."[16]

There were also hearty feasting and drinking for three days running, in the old princely tradition. The heroes loved pleasures as much as arduous tasks. Anglo-Saxon heroes like Beowulf pause neither day nor night for food or sleep in their breathless adventures. But peaks of poetic extravagance in Celtic stories are mingled again and again with a hard grip on the earth. Cuchulain, when exhausted, swore: "I would be ready to fight with any man of you if I had but my fill of food and of sleep."[17] But Emain Macha was not without its ideals. The heroes cherished nobility of birth, the independence of the free-born, courage, a fine physique, beauty and brightness of form, loyalty among friends, good sense, fair speech, and "mannerly ways." They conducted their doings with a ceremony and generosity befitting their high station.

Behind the human scene presided the Sidhe, like fate itself, meddling in the affairs of men. The Druids, too, were in evidence, dispensing wisdom and good counsel to lessen the follies and sorrows of men.

It was against such a background, close to nature and responsive to the imagination, that Yeats's plays on Cuchulain took shape. In some ways very like the material of the Noh theater, Celtic myth and history included idealism, nobility, the heroic temper, and the supernatural or ghostly world. Especially did legends of the Red Branch lend themselves to stylized stagecraft and to symbolic representation of human passions and situations. Yeats had set before himself an ideal—that of distance in art—and was progressively moving toward it in all possible ways. The Celtic subject matter gave him one kind of distance; the stylized, ritualized technique of the Noh another; symbolism gave him still a third. From these elements he created his plays for dancers. Those included in *Four Plays for Dancers* —*At the Hawk's Well, The Only Jealousy of Emer, The Dreaming of the Bones,* and *Calvary*—are closely modeled on the Noh. Others, like *The Resurrection, The Cat and the Moon* (both in prose), *A Full Moon in March,* and *The Death of Cuchulain,* have some Noh features.

At the Hawk's Well and *The Only Jealousy of Emer* merit especially close attention. Of the plays for dancers, these are the earliest experiments along Japanese lines and have all the excitement of the new; and of the five plays on Cuchulain (not all in the Noh style), these two are the most significant. I would like to examine them at some length, in terms of not only their Noh technique but also their choice of subject matter and their symbolism. This last I believe to be the subtlest of the means by which Yeats sought to achieve that blend of distance and intimacy of which he speaks so repeatedly in connection with dramatic art.

Where not otherwise indicated, the factual information in the following pages is gleaned from the 1921 Macmillan edition of *Four Plays for Dancers,* with its ample notes on production, lighting, music, masks, and acting by Yeats himself.

At the Hawk's Well, written in 1916, published in 1917, translated into Japanese in 1920, and dedicated most appropriately to Ezra Pound, has an interesting stage history. The first performance took place in London on April 2, 1916, in Lady Cunard's drawing room before a very select audience that included T. S. Eliot, Arthur Waley, and Edmund Dulac. Michio Ito, Yeats's Japanese friend, danced the part of the hawk-girl, the guardian of the well. Henry Ainley acted the part of Cuchulain. No drama critics or photographers were admitted. Yeats took great pleasure in telling a news photographer who had planted his camera in the drawing room that "we did not invite the press and that flash-light photographers were not desirable for their own sake. He [the photographer] was incredulous and persistent . . . and it was nearly ten minutes before we could persuade him to go away. What a relief after directing a theatre for so many years . . . to think no more of pictures unless Mr. Dulac or some other distinguished man had made them, nor of all those paragraphs written by young men, perhaps themselves intelligent, who must applaud the common taste or starve."[18]

The second performance took place two days later, also in London, this time in Lady Islington's drawing room at Chesterfield Gardens, with Queen Alexandria and three hundred members of the social and intellectual elite present. The aristocratic audience perhaps bore some resemblance to the patrician spectators at the Noh plays performed before Japanese shoguns in an earlier age. Ten years later the play was produced in Dublin in Yeats's own drawing room and generated the same excitement as its first performance.[19] In November and December 1939 it was presented in Japan by Michio Ito and others. Still later it was rewritten in Japanese as a Noh play and staged in Tokyo on October 20, 1949, with music by a leading Noh actor, Minoru Kita. The play was performed in English at the Suidobashi Nohgakudo in Tokyo as recently as December 12, 1972. Nor are these the only occasions on which At the Hawk's Well has been staged.

At its first performance the play was acted in a stylized manner on a bare stage. Against an austerely patterned screen designed by Edmund Dulac, of black cloth on which is painted the awe-inspiring figure of an enormous gold hawk, its wings brooding ominously over the whole scene, the three musicians, faces made up to resemble masks, and moving like marionettes, unfold and fold a cloth on which Dulac designed another pattern suggesting a gold hawk. This takes the place of the rising of the curtain before the play begins. Much care is taken to present the background not as a distracting landscape but as a canvas for a portrait, with a single color. The guardian of the well, whose face is also painted to resemble a mask, and who wears a hawk costume designed by Gordon Craig and is shrouded in a black cloak, crouches near the well. The well, "long choked up and dry,"[20] is represented by a square of blue cloth. The rest of the scene is left to the imagination and to descriptions in the opening lyrics and songs. The musicians also take care of hand properties.

Briefly stated, the plot presents Cuchulain's quest for the waters of immortality and youth and shows how he and an old man who had waited for the same waters are foiled in their attempt by the cruel enchantment of the vengeful Sidhe. According to Peter Ure, in his book *Yeats the Playwright,* the theme of the play is courage.[21] However, I think there are other possible interpretations.

The play opens with songs sung by the musicians without accompaniment (the music for all the songs and for the dance finale was written by Edmund Dulac, as that for *The Dreaming of the Bones* was written by Walter Rummel). A distinction is made between music of tone and music of speech. The goal of the composers, to use Rummel's words, was "to find some tone formula which would enhance and bring out a music underlying the words."[22] The songs in *At the Hawk's Well* explain the initial situation and describe the landscape:

> I call to the eye of the mind
> A well long choked up and dry
> And boughs long stripped by the wind,
> . . . .
> The boughs of the hazel shake,
> The sun goes down in the west.
> . . . .
> Night falls;
> The mountain-side grows dark . . .

"The hazels drop their nuts and withered leaves" among the barren stones around the well. The reference to the hazel is important. It is the Irish tree of life and knowledge and is a symbol of quest. Two contradictory aspects of the quest are neatly given in the lines "The heart would be always awake, / The heart would turn to its rest."

The weariness of the seeker is represented by the old man, who has been on his quest for the last fifty years. He wears a mask designed to emphasize the "pallor of an ivory face." Doubled up, climbing marionettelike among gray boulders, he shivers in the cold of the autumn evening and lights a fire of sticks. In spite of the advice of the chorus—"Why wander and nothing to find?/Better grow old and sleep"—he keeps himself doggedly and painfully awake. His sole companion all day long is the silent, unanswering spirit of the well. The theme of weariness is repeated in the picture of this hawk-girl, who has been guarding the waters, it seems, from the beginning of time and is "worn out from gathering up the leaves." The old man complains that she has not uttered a word since the day before. She is "stupid as a fish," not "pleasant and companionable." Her eyes are ominously dazed and heavy. She puts on that glassy countenance whenever the spring is about to gush forth. This drives the old man crazy with fear and anxiety lest he miss again the chance to drink the life-giving water.

The weariness of the quest is offset by the zest and urgency of the young man, who "rose from table, . . . spread sail," and "found this shore." He wears a noble mask. "Glittering in [his] coat," with "gold/On head and feet," he makes a sudden and dazzling entry. One can see that he is himself dazzled by a vision of the heroic life and is carried away by the impetuosity of youth. He pompously announces that he is the renowned Cuchulain, son of Sualtim. A summons had led him (actually he is led by the hawk, the spirit of the well) to seek a well wherein

> Three hazels drop their nuts and withered leaves,
> And where a solitary girl keeps watch
> Among grey boulders.

He has heard that whoever drinks of the miraculous waters lives forever. Cuchulain says he sees the three stripped hazels, the boulders, and the solitary guardian, but no well. The old man replies that he has never heard of the renowned Cuchulain and mocks the arrogance and folly of youth:

> And do you think so great a gift is found
> By no more toil than spreading out a sail,
> And climbing a steep hill? . . .
> Why should that hollow place fill for you,
> That will not fill for me?

Inhospitable and grudging, the old man informs Cuchulain that the waters are guarded by the spirit of the well and that they bubble up only fitfully and are gone before one can take a sip. They have cheated him thrice since he first came to the well "young in body and mind" but withered now. Cuchulain is undaunted by this piece of discouraging news and resolves: "I will stand here and wait. . . . My luck is strong. . . . If I grow drowsy I can pierce my foot."

The old man roughly tries to dissuade Cuchulain from his mission, partly to eliminate competition with a strenuous young man, partly to warn Cuchulain against the delusions and curses of the Sidhe woman. He says he can sense by the behavior of the girl, especially her shivering, that the water is about to bubble forth. Whereupon Cuchulain, hero-fashion, offers every courtesy to the old man and promises to share the water with him. All through this altercation the hawk's inauspicious cry is heard at intervals and momentarily unsettles the young man. He recalls how on his way to the well an extraordinary and fearsome bird had swooped down upon him to tear him with its beak.

Now the guardian of the well throws off her cloak and is seen in her costume suggesting a hawk. She fixes her "unmoistened eyes," the "eyes of a hawk," upon Cuchulain, but Cuchulain defiantly proceeds to the well and sits down:

I am not afraid of you, bird, woman, or witch.
Do what you will, I shall not leave this place
Till I have grown immortal like yourself.

While the musicians are singing, the silent girl begins her dance with hawklike movements. She dances so ravishingly and casts such a spell that the old man dozes off and the young man, "madness . . . laid hold upon him," grows pale, staggers to his feet, and in a trance-like dance pursues the girl. In the meantime the sound of water splashing is heard. Cuchulain hears it and sees the water glittering among the stones. The girl leaves. Cuchulain drops his spear as if in a dream and follows. As in the Noh, the visionary world created by the last dance dissolves. The old man wakes up, and curses and laments his wasted life. Cuchulain, still in pursuit of the maiden, returns to the well and finds her gone. Both the old man and the young are outwitted by the cruel spirit of the well. Both are bewitched and torn away from their central quest. But at the same time, and as a result of the loss, both gain better knowledge of and control over themselves.

The musicians then announce the arrival of Aoife and her troop, "the fierce women of the hills," who have been aroused against Cuchulain by the guardian of the well. Cuchulain knows that a "clash of arms" is at hand. No longer in a dream, he shoulders his spear and, true to his passionate nature, rushes out, calling: "I will face them./He comes! Cuchulain, son of Sualtim, comes!"

This is the end of Cuchulain's vivid adventure at the well. He had come with a trembling upon him of things undreamed of by mortals, to do battle with the mountain women and with his fate. The process of Cuchulain's further self-discovery has begun, to be continued in *The Only Jealousy of Emer*. The play ends with the unfolding and folding of the cloth. The last lyric sums up the theme: "Wisdom must live a bitter life."

As in the Noh, the play consists of a dialogue, here between the old man and the young man. There is no ghost in this play, though the old man is a kind of shadow of his former self and the hawk-girl partakes of the supernatural. The old man relates the story and the young man for the most part listens. The girl's role is to dance. But this slender drama rests upon sustained symbolism. Cuchulain is a symbol of the instinctive, passionate life. The old man represents the life of the intellect, not necessarily debility and physical decay. Despite the infirmities of old age he speaks and acts with spirit and hope. Each, complementing the other, strives for the same thing: the fullest possible life, beyond the reach of mortality—a wisdom of the head and heart, which in the ideal man, according to Yeats, is a synthesis of opposites—the self and the antiself.

The play contains many symbols. Water stands for immortality or wisdom, the wisdom of the "unageing intellect" that we later find in Yeats's Byzantium poems. The hazel again suggests knowledge, wisdom. It is also the tree of life. The number three (three hazels) lends a mystical touch. All earthly delusions, accidents, and ironies of life are indicated by the prominent symbol of the hawk. As Peter Ure says: "The hawk is a delusion that attracts and destroys." Cuchulain's dance under the spell of the hawk-girl means that momentarily he has lost his vision of the well and all that it stands for. But when the battle cry sounds in his ears he is roused, he is restored and leaves to fulfill his destiny in a life of action. The old man in *At the Hawk's Well* very wisely says to the young man, Cuchulain: "And never till you are lying in the earth / Can you know rest." And truly, to his dying day he does not know rest.

In "The Wanderings of Oisin," a poem about the son of the fabled Finn and of the Fianna of the halls of Tara, who belonged to the heroic cycle of Irish legend following the age of Cuchulain, Yeats had been preoccupied with the same theme of immortality. Immortal Niamh, with whom Oisin sojourned in the Land of the Ever-Young, is a symbol of intense spiritual life, and Oisin longs to conquer time, death, and change. But he is defeated in his enterprise because of his homesickness for Ireland. The moment he sets foot in his native land, which is "no longer now the happy pagan country of his youth three hundred years ago," hoary age descends upon him. The tyranny of the temporal world bows him down. Looking around, he finds that his sole companion is Saint Patrick, the patron saint of Ireland, with the Irish people preoccupied with religion, prayer, and penance. Intense spiritual experience in "The Wanderings of Oisin" and intense passion in *At the Hawk's Well* are represented by symbols.

Two verse styles are noticeable in *At the Hawk's Well*. The lyrics are as beautiful as those found in the other three plays in *Four Plays for Dancers*. The imagery is repeated in delightfully varying patterns, with key words and lines unchanged. Where a symbolic content is necessary the poetry is lofty or wistful. But dialogue contributing to the action of the play is direct, bare of ornament and characteristic of the speaker. For instance, the old man is impolite, almost rude. He addresses Cuchulain impatiently: "There is no house to sack among these hills / Nor beautiful woman to be carried off." And Cuchulain observes brightly: "You should be a native here, for that rough tongue / Matches the barbarous spot." The dialogue is speedy, but the lyrics are full of brooding pauses so that the symbolism can create the mood of the poetic experience. The following lullaby to the soul in the early part of the play is charged with the meaning of Cuchulain's adventure, his journey to the well:

> 'O wind, O salt wind, O sea wind!'
> Cries the heart, 'It is time to sleep;
> Why wander and nothing to find?'

The last chorus of the three musicians ruminates on the pursuit of wisdom:

> Folly alone I cherish,
> I choose it for my share;
> Being but a mouthful of air,
> I am content to perish;
> I am but a mouthful of sweet air.
>
> O lamentable shadows,
> Obscurity of strife!
> I choose a pleasant life,
> Among indolent meadows;
> Wisdom must live a bitter life.
>   . . . .
> 'The man that I praise',
> Cries out the leafless tree,
> 'Has married and stays
> By an old hearth, and he
> On naught has set store
> But children and dogs on the floor.
> Who but an idiot would praise
> A withered tree?'

The Only Jealousy of Emer, written between 1917 and 1918 and published in 1919, is Yeats's second play for dancers. Though the story has been considerably changed in the dramatization, it is based on the chapter called "The Only Jealousy of Emer" in Lady Gregory's *Cuchulain of Muirthemne.*

Cuchulain in this play has come a long way from the days of his impetuous, heady youth, when he had come to drink the immortal waters at the hawk's well. He has been fulfilling his destiny. He has fought many battles and severed many heads, and Ireland is in dread of the strength of his arm. He has proved not only his heroism but his integrity and courage. In *The Green Helmet,* a heroic farce, where the quarrel among Cuchulain, Conall, and Laegaire for first place in the kingdom has comic reverberations among the wives of the heroes, the stable boys, and the scullions, Yeats shows that Cuchulain is not only the "cock of the yard" as Laeg, his charioteer, calls him, but the only one of the three top men of Ulster who does not flinch from keeping his word even at the risk of his life. Cuchulain has feasted and played hero-games and has had many loves. Eithne Inguba says to Cuchulain: "There is not a woman of them but would share her love and friendship with you."[23] He has married Emer of the Yellow Hair. He has also suffered, chiefly through vicious women and jealous gods. It was through the plotting of the boastful power-fiend, Queen Maeve of Cruachan, that he killed his best friend, Ferdiad, and was stricken with grief many days. In Yeats's play *On Baile's Strand* it was through the vengefulness of Aoife, Queen of Alban, that he unwittingly killed his one and only son and was utterly cast down by sorrow and sickness.

The events leading up to *The Only Jealousy of Emer* are dramatized in *On Baile's Strand*. In fact in Yeats's prose version of *The Only Jealousy of Emer*, entitled *Fighting the Waves*, the curtain at the back of the stage was to be a seascape suggesting the waves with which Cuchulain had fought for three days, maddened by grief and remorse for having killed his son.

In *The Only Jealousy of Emer* gods and humans alike contend for the soul of Cuchulain. As the play opens Cuchulain, having been overcome by the waves, is lying in a deathlike enchantment exercised by a woman of the Sidhe who is really Fand of the Country-under-Wave. She is in love with Cuchulain and longs for him to stay with her in the sea kingdom. She is the temptress who offers Cuchulain immortal love, her nonhuman love. Bricriu, also of the Sidhe, on the other hand, hates Fand and is seeking revenge on her by keeping Cuchulain separated from her. As the play opens Emer, Cuchulain's wife, with the help of his young mistress, Eithne Inguba, is trying desperately to recall Cuchulain's soul and bring him back to life. Bricriu bargains with Emer, promising to return Cuchulain to life if she will forfeit her dearest wish, to have her husband back at her hearth someday. After much struggle Emer decides to perform this heroic sacrifice. In the end both Emer and the woman of the Sidhe lose Cuchulain, who despite his great love for Emer falls into the arms of his mistress, Eithne Inguba, as soon as he is restored to life.

A Noh play usually has two scenes — although they are not necessarily divided or marked as separate scenes—and the climax is reached in the second, in the visionary world of dream and dance. *The Only Jealousy of Emer* has three scenes (though they are not marked as separate scenes), which dissolve one into another. First there is the routine, everyday world in the poor fisherman's hut, with Cuchulain lying half dead and Emer and Eithne Inguba trying to revive him; then the visionary ghost world from which Eithne Inguba recoils in horror, characterized by the dance around Cuchulain's ghost by the masked and metallic woman of the Sidhe. This is followed by the everyday world again when Cuchulain recovers from his state of collapse and cries out: "Your arms, your arms! O Eithne Inguba, /I have been in some strange place and am afraid." True to his Irish, or more correctly Western European, character, Cuchulain throws off the enchantment of the visionary world and returns to the actual world of love and women and action. A similar return is suggested in *At the Hawk's Well* when Cuchulain, the man of action, returns to a life of battle after the enchantment of the hawk-girl's dance. *The Dreaming of the Bones* ends more like the Noh, with a dance, leaving one with a sense of questioning and wistfulness.

The dramatis personae in *The Only Jealousy of Emer* include three musicians with faces made up to resemble masks, the ghost of Cuchulain, and the figure of Cuchulain (actually Bricriu in disguise), both wearing masks. Emer and Eithne Inguba are masked or have their faces painted to resemble masks, and the woman of the Sidhe (Fand) also wears a mask, with metallic glitter in her hair and costume to give the impression of an idol.

The play opens with the unfolding and folding of the cloth to the accompaniment of a chant by the first musician in the exquisite lyric that begins:

A woman's beauty is like a white
Frail bird, like a white sea-bird alone
At daybreak after stormy night
Between two furrows upon the ploughed land . . .

The first musician also describes the initial situation and the scene, a poor fisherman's house, where Cuchulain, reclaimed from the sea, lies on a curtained litter in grave-clothes and heroic mask. Another man in identical grave-clothes and mask crouches near the front. Emer sits beside the bed and is present on the stage throughout as a witness to the events, as in the Noh the priest is a witness to the events in the protagonist's life story. Emer, putting away her wifely pride, half-entreats and half-challenges Eithne Inguba, Cuchulain's mistress, to release the swooning man from the power of the Sidhe and recall him to life, while Emer herself throws new logs upon the hearth to chase away the evil spell of old Manannan the sea god, Fand's husband, who, it is believed, dreads hearth fire. Emer is certain that Cuchulain is not dead. The great hero could not die without ceremony. As Emer says: "The very heavens when that day's at hand,/ . . . Will throw out fires." His death will be "like the world's end." She covers her husband's face and asks Eithne Inguba to approach him: "I am but his wife, but if you cry aloud/With the sweet voice that is so dear to him/He cannot help but listen./ . . . Call out dear secrets till you have touched his heart, / . . . Then kiss that image. . . ."

When Eithne Inguba approaches Cuchulain's lips she starts back, shuddering at the touch of the figure's withered arm, and discovers that she has touched Bricriu, who has taken the shape and form of Cuchulain. The bargaining that follows between Emer and Bricriu for the soul of Cuchulain is subtle and full of dramatic appeal:

FIGURE OF CUCHULAIN.   You have but to pay the price and he
  is free.
EMER. Do the Sidhe bargain? . . .
FIGURE OF CUCHULAIN.   You have but to put yourself into
  that power
  And he shall live again.

EMER.   No, never, never. . . .
>   I have but two joyous thoughts, two things I prize,
>   A hope, a memory, and now you claim that hope.

The figure of Cuchulain replies vindictively and prophetically:

>   He'll never sit beside you at the hearth
>   Or make old bones, but die of wounds and toil
>   On some far shore or mountain, a strange woman
>   Beside his mattress.

During the dialogue between Emer and Bricriu the woman of
the Sidhe, with her mask and costume that suggest glittering gold,
begins to dance in an ever-increasing tempo around the ghost of Cuchulain. The wooing of Cuchulain by the Sidhe woman rises to a
crescendo of success. As their lips are about to meet, Cuchulain
remembers Emer, his "lost Emer," and he is torn between his
fidelity to his wife and his attraction to the Sidhe woman—a mere
delusion. This happens twice, but Cuchulain is caught in such thrall
that he is unable to free himself. It is at this point that Emer is driv-
en to accept Bricriu's bargain and to make her renunciation. Now
Emer's only wish is that her husband be set free from the cruel grip
of death. "A wise silence" falls in the dark,[24] the spell of the
dance is broken, and Cuchulain's ghost leaves. The Sidhe woman,
bereft of her prize, turns to Bricriu with mocking, sour words: "To
you that have no living light, being dropped/From a last leprous
crescent of the moon,/I owe it all."[25]

The figure of Cuchulain falls back on the bed and behind the curtain changes his mask for a heroic mask. Now very slowly Cuchulain
awakes and his body is revived. As the woman of the Sidhe retreats,
Eithne Inguba approaches Cuchulain and he falls into her arms, never
realizing that he owes his life to Emer, whom he has rejected twice,
first in favor of the Sidhe woman and now in favor of Eithne Inguba.

The play ends with the song "O Bitter Reward"—Emer's reward
and Fand's reward. While Fand goes back to the sea kingdom, Emer
returns to her noble house, to live as the first lady of the land, envied
by women, possessing honor, wealth, beauty, and a name—but not
Cuchulain.

Among the heroines of modern poetic drama Ibsen's Solvig in *Peer Gynt*, Synge's Deirdre in *Deirdre of the Sorrows,* and Yeats's Emer in *The Only Jealousy of Emer* to my mind have the quality of the poetic and the tragic sublime. All three women annihilated themselves for love. Solvig's eyes grew lusterless and old with waiting for Peer by the door of her hut in the remote hills in order that Peer, the lost one, might return and be found by her. The fate of Deirdre of the House of Usnach was both tragic and enviable. Seven long glad years with Naoise in the wild woods of Scotland were enough for any mortal's share of happiness. Her death saved her from old Conchubar, king of Ulster, who coveted her, and also from disenchantment in love. Deirdre had already sensed, partly by eavesdropping when Naoise was discussing his return to Ulster, that his love would cool under stress. Emer's lot was the hardest of the three. Emptied of hope, she had only a happy memory to mock her all her days. Irony and bewilderment converge to an intense pitch in the last song of the musicians in *The Only Jealousy of Emer,* sung as they unfold and fold the cloth; and yet this song has a strange power to still the heart:

> O bitter reward
> Of many a tragic tomb!
> And we though astonished are dumb
> Or give but a sigh and a word,
> A passing word.

> What makes your heart so beat?
> What man is at your side?
> When beauty is complete
> Your own thought will have died
> And danger not be diminished;
> Dimmed at three-quarter light,
> When moon's round is finished
> The stars are out of sight.

> O bitter reward
> Of many a tragic tomb!
> And we though astonished are dumb

> Or give but a sigh and a word,
> A passing word.

The last two lines with their repetition of "word" recall the musical echo of Noh poetry. When the curtain is folded again, the stage is bare.

This play embodies one or more of Yeats's central beliefs. In the preface to *Four Plays for Dancers* he writes: "*The Only Jealousy of Emer* was written to find out what dramatic effect one could get out of a mask changed while the player remains upon the stage to suggest a change of personality."[26] Yeats's preoccupation with the dual nature of personality is also seen in the creation of that famous pair Michael Robartes and Owen Aherne. In "The Trembling of the Veil" Yeats writes: "My mind began drifting vaguely towards that doctrine of the mask which has convinced me that every passionate man is, as it were, linked with another age, historical or imaginary, where alone he finds images that rouse his energy."[27]

In *At the Hawk's Well* Cuchulain and the old man, representing passion and reason respectively, are two sides of the same person. In *The Only Jealousy of Emer*, as we have seen, the figure of Cuchulain, when Eithne Inguba tries to awaken it by a kiss, turns out to be Bricriu of the Sidhe. (This is shown by changing the heroic mask of Cuchulain for the distorted one of the figure of Cuchulain—Bricriu— behind the curtain of the bed.) The figure of Cuchulain starts up, saying: "I show my face and everything he loves/Must fly away." Discord and devastation follow in Bricriu's wake. Toward the end of the play, after the woman of the Sidhe and Bricriu leave the stage, the figure of Cuchulain is transformed into Cuchulain himself, wearing the hero-mask and calling out: "Your arms, your arms! O Eithne Inguba,/I have been in some strange place and am afraid."

Pondering the significance of change in Cuchulain's personality, I venture the observation that Cuchulain is both fate and the mocker of fate, destroyer of value. In other words, man has infinite possibilities to make his own destiny and to order his life's pattern. But at the same time weaknesses and passions inherent in human nature thwart and mock at the course he would take. The villain is within.

It is not really Bricriu. Yeats has presented an inner conflict symbolically. As quoted earlier, "All the gains of man come from conflict
with the opposite of his being." A character on the stage comes alive
when visualized through conflict with other characters in the play.
Iago and Othello are two different characters, but according to Maud
Bodkin in *Archetypal Patterns in Poetry* they are really counterparts of
the same personality. Faust and Mephistopheles, again according to
Maud Bodkin, are also one and the same personality representing
inner contradictions. Iago and Mephistopheles threaten the values
that Othello and Faust hold most dear. In *The Only Jealousy of Emer*
this same conflict is dramatized by a change of mask. Here Bricriu
and Cuchulain are one. It was not an external agent that turned Cuchulain away from his loyalty to Emer. It was in his nature to turn
to other women. He was the amorous man par excellence.

In *The Green Helmet,* when Cuchulain is about to sacrifice his life to
keep his word of honor, Emer begins to keen before she draws her
dagger to put an end to her life. Cuchulain then consoles her with
these words: "Little wife, little wife, be at rest." He continues in
the following vein: "You are young, you are wise, you can call/
Some kinder and comelier man that will sit in the house." Emer replies: "Live and be faithless still." To be a rover and to be "faithless still" is his necessity, and the wise woman who loves him knows
and accepts.

The woman of the Sidhe is a deception, a "body of air," whom
the knife of Emer cannot hurt but who can draw Cuchulain into her
glittering basket "with dreams upon the hook." Cuchulain himself
recognizes her as that "half woman and half bird of prey" who had
eluded him at the hawk's well. He will have nothing of her now that
he is no longer "the young and passionate man [he] was." He knows
now that there is "folly in the deathless Sidhe," who are beyond
man's reach; for they, not being human, cannot know what Cuchulain now knows—that men and women are held together in love and
loyalty not only through joyous experiences but more, perhaps,
through the pain and suffering they bring into one another's lives.
Here Cuchulain makes another kind of self-discovery.

The most interesting of Yeats's beliefs expressed in this play con-

cerns the nature of woman's beauty. His convictions on this subject
are found in *A Vision* in a complicated and elaborate theory of the
subjective and objective types of personality. In a note on *The Only
Jealousy of Emer,* Yeats writes: "I have filled *The Only Jealousy of Emer*
with those little-known convictions about the nature and history of
a woman's beauty. . . . The soul through each cycle of its development is held to incarnate through twenty-eight typical incarnations
corresponding to the phases of the moon, the light part of the moon's
disc symbolising the subjective and the dark part the objective
nature."[28] In these twenty-eight phases every possible type of
human intellect and beauty is possible. Phase one and phase fifteen
symbolize complete objectivity and complete subjectivity respectively, but these have no human characteristics, nor are they visible to
human eyes. The invisible fifteenth incarnation is that of the greatest
possible beauty and perfection and the fourteenth and the sixteenth
those of the greatest beauty and perfection visible to the human eye.
But "objective natures are declared to be always ugly, hence the dis-
agreeable appearance of politicians, philanthropists, reformers and
men of science."[29] Bricriu, an objective type, has a distorted face.
He has "no living light." He is dropped "from a last leprous crescent of the moon." This is a reference to the period of decadence in
the historical cycle, when corruption and evil abound and which
produces ugly natures.

In Yeats's system, beauty is no free bounty of God or chance. It is
the result of emotional toil in past lives and is possible only to subjective natures. A saint and a woman of great beauty are symbols of
the victory of the soul. If we want to, we can see here the influence of
Indian thought in the doctrine of karma and the transmigration of
souls, where according to the most orthodox interpretation, chiefly
in Jainism, the soul passes almost mechanically through hundreds of
incarnations before it reaches perfection, at which point the soul
ceases to exist as a separate entity and experiences Nirvana, that is,
release from the bondage of birth and death: "I am nothing, for I am
all." Yeats does not go quite that far. He finds a satisfying philosophy
of personality before reaching the Indian point of extinction and
bliss. In Yeats's system the march toward perfection is a conscious

one. It means toil. It is not mechanical. This idea corresponds to the more lofty interpretation in the *Upanishads* of the same Indian doctrine of karma and transmigration of souls, where the will and volition and works of man are crucial in placing him in the higher or lower scales of existence. Man thus becomes his own agent in the cosmic ladder of development and is responsible for all his moral choices and acts.

Yeats had an intuitive feeling that Maud Gonne's soul was distinguished and subtle as exhibited in her great physical beauty. His romantic image of Maud Gonne is relevant to his conception of female characters in *The Only Jealousy of Emer*. "She [Maud Gonne] looked as though she lived in an ancient civilization. . . . Her whole body seemed a master-work of long labouring thought, as though a Scopas had measured and calculated, consorted with Egyptian sages and mathematicians out of Babylon, that he might outface even Artemisia's sepulchral image with a living norm."[30]

In the opening lines of *The Only Jealousy of Emer* Yeats emphasizes two things. The first is the frailty and transient nature of woman's beauty. These are expressed through the imagery of sea birds and seashells:

> A woman's beauty is like a white
> Frail bird, like a white sea-bird alone
> At daybreak after stormy night
> Between two furrows upon the ploughed land:
> . . . .
> A strange, unserviceable thing,
> A fragile, exquisite, pale shell,
> That the vast troubled waters bring
> To the loud sands before day has broken.

Bird symbolism in Yeats is significant. A bird is usually a symbol of a subjective nature unless it is a cock, as in *The Dreaming of the Bones,* where the red cock, the red bird of March, means betrayal. Birds in *Calvary* also represent subjectivity. The golden bird of Byzantium means artifice.

The second emphasis is on the discipline, the "bloody press," the

exacting mathematical accuracy, and above all the "emotional toil"
of centuries, the violence and suffering that have gone into the
creation of a lovely form:

> How many centuries spent
> The sedentary soul
> In toils of measurement
> Beyond eagle or mole,
> Beyond hearing or seeing,
> Or Archimedes' guess,
> To raise into being
> That loveliness?
>
> . . . .
>
> What death? what discipline?
> What bonds no man could unbind,
> Being imagined within
> The labyrinth of the mind,
> What pursuing or fleeing,
> What wounds, what bloody press,
> Dragged into being
> This loveliness?

This is what seems to have gone into the making also of Blake's tiger
burning bright in the forests of the night.

In *The Only Jealousy of Emer* there are three women, all of indescribable beauty and brightness of form. The woman of the Sidhe, a half-
divine being, is incomparable in beauty. Strangely enough, she is the
only one whose appearance is at all described, though the description is indirect. Eithne Inguba is only a little less beautiful, and Emer
of the Yellow Hair is beautiful, too. To which of these three is it that
Yeats's lines on beauty refer—or is it to all of them? It is not Cuchulain but his ghost that sees the woman of the Sidhe as perfection in beauty when she dances around him to awaken him:

> Who is it stands before me there
> Shedding such light from limb and hair
> As when the moon, complete at last
> With every labouring crescent past,

And lonely with extreme delight,
Flings out upon the fifteenth night?

This is Cuchulain's partial illusion because he is a ghost at that time and therefore can see the invisible. The woman of the Sidhe says to him: "Because I long I am not complete." She still retains something of the human, but there remains only an hour or so to complete the round of her journey and to bring her into the fifteenth phase. She pleads with Cuchulain for his love:

> Could you that have loved many a woman
> That did not reach beyond the human,
> Lacking a day to be complete,
> Love one that, though her heart can beat,
> Lacks it but by an hour or so?

Both Eithne Inguba and the woman of the Sidhe belong to the fourteenth phase, where the highest possible visible beauty is attainable. One needs only a day and the other only an hour to pass beyond the human into the completely spiritual. Eithne Inguba is the more human. The opening lines on woman's beauty must then refer to her rather than to the woman of the Sidhe, who is more a supernatural being than a woman, besides which she is an illusion. In Emer's blunt language, she "Has hid herself in this disguise and made/ Herself into a lie."

The poet images to himself a woman of perfect beauty partly for beauty's sake; but chiefly because a woman is a part of man, if man is to be a complete being, and thus she fulfills a deep-felt inner need. Eve, Helen, Beatrice, and Margaret are projections of their creators' ideals of feminine perfection; each complements the creator's own personality, which in its fullness is a composite of the male and the female principles in life. In *The Only Jealousy of Emer* all three women are symbols of beauty, refinement, and the good. Each satisfies some aspect of man's desire for completion. Emer's sweetness, loyalty, and domesticity; the spirituality, intensity, and unearthliness of Fand (the woman of the Sidhe); Eithne Inguba's physical passion and loveliness are all embodiments of a perfect woman. But what woman is fortunate enough to combine all these aspects in a single image of perfection in a single paltry lifetime?

My attempt to disentangle abstractions from situation and character in this play in order to answer the logic of the mind should not be carried too far, however. Yeats's plays for dancers create their own response, for their appeal is directly to the primary emotions and passions of man presented symbolically. They resolve the paradoxes and complexities of life and increase their poignancy and power through the beauty of a disciplined artistic form. The ritualistic enraptured dances, the lyrics of swift and momentary impulse caught in words of surpassing aptness and delicacy, the sustained symbolism, the technique of the Noh and the stark stage, the stylized movements and gestures, the brevity of action and intensity of passion contribute to the total effect and make these plays unique in the history of poetic drama.

Six   EVALUATION : HINTS
OF A SECRET SOCIETY

More miracle than bird or handiwork . . .

YEATS HAD NEVER SEEN THE NOH acted in its original home and
setting. Those were not the days of quick, easy air travel between
distant countries. Yet Yeats came remarkably near capturing much of
the artistic form and some of the spirit of the Japanese classical theater. Whether he was successful from the point of view of permanent-
ly capturing and engaging the attention of the Western playgoer and
the Western critic is another matter. The publication of *Four Plays
for Dancers* in 1921 was decidedly a piece of exciting theater news and
gave rise to diverse and spirited points of view. Here was something
entirely out of line with the Western theater tradition. Its reception
was mixed. The press in England and the United States buzzed with
rumor and report. I have included in the Bibliography references to
some of the many reviews that appeared in rapid succession in 1921
and 1922. There is much entertaining material in the then current
periodicals as well as in later criticism both shrewd and whimsical.
I would like to give below a sampling of this criticism on the much
discussed subject of Yeats's dramatic talent and technique as seen in
his *Four Plays for Dancers.*
    Some thought Yeats's experiment was farfetched, was nonsense as

drama. Others thought Yeats was a great dramatist. Louis MacNeice wrote in *The Poetry of W. B. Yeats:* "Yeats was a cause of drama in others . . . but not a dramatist himself."[1] MacNeice found Yeats's plays less original, less powerful, less interesting than his poetry. He writes about *Four Plays for Dancers* that they had no psychology, no characterization, no comedy, and no contemporary life, being drawn from legend. "Action is eliminated," passion and motive are everything, and all is "subordinated to a unity of feeling and mood."[2] Yeats's dramatic failure is attributed by MacNeice to the typical Irish temperament, and his plays are all but dismissed as "charades." In his book MacNeice is primarily interested in Yeats as a lyrical poet. It is not surprising, therefore, that the plays are only summarily treated in a brief survey. But as will be seen below, there is sound criticism in some of what he says.

The *Yale Review* was very caustic. The October 1922 issue carried one short paragraph by O. W. Firkins on *Four Plays for Dancers.* Firkins is impatient with Yeats for not being the poet that he was, for concerning himself with eccentric dramatic technique instead of writing poetry—a point of view similar to that of MacNeice. Firkins asks: "Why all this adaptation of remote erudition to dramatize eccentricity? The poet has a scholar at one elbow and a stage director at the other; neither arm is quite free to move."[3] But the most astonishing thing that Firkins says is that Yeats was writing for a theater company. This is, to say the least, wide of the mark. *Four Plays for Dancers* was written, as Yeats said himself, for lovers of poetry. The scholar, the sculptor, the musician gave their services gratis, and with much pleasure, to a new enterprise and to the execution of a novel dramatic form. In fact, Yeats was proud that he was free to create as he pleased. His reference to the press and photographers, noted in chapter five, and his letter to Lady Gregory, which will be quoted below, are ample evidence of his daring license in innovation. Firkins's judgment betrays a hasty reading of the plays, perhaps for an impending review.

Edmund Wilson, in the *Freeman's Journal* of March 1922, writes: "Yeats lacks the knack of manipulating climax and surprise which makes a dramatist something different from a writer of fiction." But he goes on to find "undercurrents of profounder meaning and a sense of secrets withheld."[4] However, he leaves the secrets tantalizingly unexplored.

In later criticism Lennox Robinson, on the other hand, is far more startling. He seems to throw out an angry challenge: "The man who says Yeats is not a dramatist is a fool."[5] This sentence comes from his essay on Yeats in *Scattering Branches,* a collection of tributes to the memory of W. B. Yeats published the year after the poet's death by people who had personally known the poet. Tributes on significant calendar dates are likely to be extravagant and admirers are likely to be carried away by an extraordinary warmth of feeling hurled in defiance, as it were, of death.

In the same book there is, however, a relatively balanced estimate of Yeats's *Four Plays for Dancers* by L. A. G. Strong. Strong admits that Yeats's drama is not a stage success in the ordinary sense because there is no conflict, no character. But he acknowledges Yeats's intention, that is, that a play is not observation but a symbolic revelation of some basic human experience, in dealing with which Strong thinks that Yeats shows a "terrific sense of reality."[6]

The *Saturday Review of Literature* of December 1921 had an essay called "The Wizardry of Mr. Yeats: *Four Plays for Dancers.*" Here the lyric poetry of Yeats is praised as "more refined, more chaste, more aerial" than the poetry of his drama. The music of these plays, the writer says, "moves not like the wind, but the ghost of a wind . . . [it] breathes through a flute made out of the thigh-bone of a heron." But, he continues, the plays "place us in a world on the farther side of the tragic reality. . . . We are in no carnal world, we are in a valley of shades, and the passions of these creatures are not our own, they are alien passions we are sometimes aware of for one transitory white moment of awakening."[7]

An apt answer to this would be a statement made in the article "*Four Plays for Dancers* by Yeats" in the *Times Literary Supplement* of December 15, 1921. This careful reviewer writes: "The plays withdraw you from the world of direct and perhaps brutal events and passions away into a reality that only seems unreal because of the infinite possibilities which it is summoned to suggest. . . . The result is a greater measure of unity in drama than drama can usually achieve.''[8]

On the whole, critics expected and demanded what Yeats had not set out to do. But what had Yeats set out to do? I quote from his essay "A People's Theatre: A Letter to Lady Gregory," published in 1919. "We set out to make a 'People's Theatre' and in that we have succeeded. But I did not know until very lately that there are certain things, dear to both our hearts, which no 'People's Theatre' can accomplish. I want to create for myself an unpopular theatre and an audience like a secret society where admission is by favour and never to many. Perhaps I shall never create it. . . . However, there are my *Four Plays for Dancers* as a beginning, some masks by Mr. Dulac, music by Mr. Dulac and Mr. Rummell. . . . I desire a mysterious art, always reminding and half reminding those who understand it of dearly loved things, doing its work by suggestion, not by direct statement, a complexity of rhythm, colour, gesture, not space-pervading, like the intellect, but a memory and a prophecy. . . . I . . . must draw an outline about the things I seek; and say that I seek, not a theatre but the theatre's anti-self, an art that can appease all within us, that becomes uneasy as the curtain falls and the house breaks into applause.''[9] So there are many ways of looking at Yeats's *Four Plays for Dancers*.

In the classical tradition, plot occupies a central place. Aristotle lays stress on action in serious drama, for he believes that without action, character cannot be portrayed. The dramatists of antiquity were given sound practical advice as to how to go about the making of a plot. In Shakespeare's plays character emerges as the supreme element in serious drama. Shakespeare gave to the theater and to literature immortal heroes—Hamlet, Macbeth, Timon, Lear. From Shakespeare's day down to that of Ibsen, O'Neill, and Miller the emphasis on character in serious Western drama has rarely shifted. But in Yeats's work neither the delineation of character (through the depiction of personal qualities or through moral choices and deliberate acts of the will) nor action is of primary importance. Critics who complain that nothing happens in *Four Plays for Dancers* are not wholly wrong. Yeats's plots are brief. Externally, little happens in

At the Hawk's Well and *The Only Jealousy of Emer.* In the former, as we have already seen, Cuchulain in search of the waters of youth and immortality (a favorite theme in Yeats's work) is thwarted in his attempt by the vindictiveness of the Sidhe; in the latter, Emer renounces desire in order to save from the clutches of death her husband, Cuchulain, who, ironically, is not in the least aware of her sacrifice. Yet inwardly, much happens to Cuchulain and to Emer. They embark on adventures, they experience heroic conflict, they love, they suffer, they make discoveries about themselves or others.

These noble figures of Irish legend become for us symbols of passionate, suffering, living humanity. The irony and the tragedy are the more profound for not being presented in a literal way. The passionate moment, the passionate crisis too full and too fugitive for literal representation, is central in these plays and is best captured, Yeats believed, in symbolic representation and poetic speech. In a realistic representation much is said and done. In a formal, symbolic one much is suggested. One significant word and one characteristic gesture can carry the burden of the whole world's sorrow or good fortune. There is no need in such a context for elaborate dramatic conflict and characterization, nor for complicated acting. But in spite of this the force and vitality of character are unmistakably present. In both *At the Hawk's Well* and *The Only Jealousy of Emer* the essential personality of Cuchulain is set forth strongly through his war with himself. Here is a memorable hero "whose life is vehement and full of pleasure as though he always remembered that it was to be soon over."[10] Moreover, it was Yeats's theory that it is only in moments of comedy that one can define character. "In the supreme moments of tragedy" passion and lyrical poetry help raise the play to great heights and give the meaning and understanding of human situations. The Noh dramatists would wholly subscribe to this view, for they also rejected character and strenuous action in favor of pure passion.

If the characterization and action in Yeats's plays are symbolic and abbreviated, the acting is still more suggestive and is conveyed largely by hint and allusion. Yeats was in favor of the dramatic pauses that Sarah Bernhardt had introduced into her acting and at which she so eminently excelled. At the first performances of *At the Hawk's Well,*

Yeats was put out that the actors and musicians wanted more gestures and actions than he allowed. Another element that Yeats under-scored for this type of drama was speech—"speech [that] had taken fire" and did not have "to compete with an orchestra."[11] Fine speech—beautiful words, each word worth its weight in gold, deliv-ered not as dialogue but almost as incantations to accompany the measured ritual movements and dances—could convey in a poetic way the qualities of the passionate moment and bring it to an emo-tional crescendo in a stylized production.

Yeats neglected one other aspect of drama. Social and political problems of the time rarely gripped him as much as they did Ibsen and Shaw and Galsworthy. For all his participation in the Irish move-ment for political liberty, as a poet Yeats remained free from the deep entanglements of society. Human values and situations moved him more than social and political relationships. In his later poetry, he seems to have moved away even from the human scene into the realm of artifice and abstraction. He believed that humanity is at its hap-piest and wisest when instead of becoming passionately involved in politics and topical social preoccupations it is related to nature and to the large sweep of history and civilizations, as is seen in "The Second Coming," "Leda and the Swan," and especially the Byzanti-um poems. This attitude was not an escape from human life and val-ues but a transmutation of these into the timeless, geometric mosaics of Byzantine art and all that they symbolized for Yeats. In his own words: "I think that in early Byzantium, maybe never before or since in recorded history, religious, aesthetic and practical life were one, that architects and artificers . . . spoke to the multitude and the few alike. The painter, the mosaic worker, the worker in gold and silver, the illuminator of sacred books were almost im-personal, . . . absorbed in their subject-matter and that the vision of a whole people . . . the work of many that seemed the work of one, that made building, picture, pattern, metalwork or rail and lamp seem but a single image."[12]

Life and art complement each other—life with its diurnal and factual concerns and art with its imaginative quality. Ultimate wis-dom, as described in Yeats's poem "Byzantium," is to proceed from a life of the senses to a life of the intellect and spirit, from "the fury and the mire of human veins," from "that gong-tormented sea," to the perfect dome of the Holy City, a territory of unaging intellect outside the flux of time and nature to be shaped and molded by "the golden smithies of the Emperor." In another sense this movement toward the territory of unaging intellect outside time and nature may refer to the artist's own life as an artist—his search for meaning, his "gaiety transfiguring all that dread," and his preoccupation with consummate craftsmanship, the "accomplished fingers" evoked in the poem "Lapis Lazuli." For the poet these are ends in themselves and offer a satisfying way of life. But what of his audience?

From the point of view of the audience there are strong reasons for the lack of popularity of Yeats's plays for dancers. In a note on *The Only Jealousy of Emer* Yeats writes rather wistfully: "They [the plays for dancers] could only succeed in a civilisation very unlike ours. . . . [They] should be written for some country where all the classes share in a half-mythical, half-philosophical folk belief, which the writer and his audience lift into a new subtlety."[13] Failing that, he admitted, in effect, the unsuitability of *Four Plays for Dancers* for a general audience by rewriting *The Only Jealousy of Emer* in prose ten years later. This version is called *Fighting the Waves*. The visionary quality, symbolism, and subtlety of the former version are reduced to their minimum. Yeats seems to have moved from the European tradition to the Noh tradition for a time and then back to the demands of his Western audience. But this concession to the playgoer should by no means be considered an admission of the lack of high poetic excellence in the plays for dancers. Rather it was the very excellence of their exquisite, highly chiseled art that left the average playgoer cold. If there were a charge of snobbery against Yeats it would be justified. Note what he writes in one of his essays: "Realism is created for the common folk and was always their peculiar delight, and it is the delight today of all those whose minds educated alone by schoolmasters and newspapers are without the memory of beauty and emotional subtlety."[14]

Yeats sought subtlety in his artistic pursuits. But it was not a matter of subtleties alone. The temperament congenial to the Noh style of art is a highly cultivated and fastidious one. The aristocrats of medieval Japan were martial in their occupation, but through training and discipline they had also acquired the detachment and sense of repose inculcated by Zen philosophy. Their natural leanings toward mundane duties and their cultivated sense of otherworldliness were welded into a new, conscious alliance that became almost a native pose. Or perhaps the two antithetical tendencies operated at different times, each sufficing for the needs of the hour. Excitement, adventure, conflict served them well as men of action on the battlefield. The Noh, the tea ceremony, Zen meditation provided periods of emotional and intellectual tranquillity for other occasions and moods. The Noh plays of Japan, Yeats's models for his plays for dancers, were indigenous products of Japan, grounded in Japanese culture and outlook, in the ritual worship of Shinto gods, and in ancestor worship.

The feudal lords, restricted in their pleasures and pastimes, as already noted, found the Noh the only form of dramatic entertainment worthy of their station and ideals. This kept the Noh very exclusive and unadulterated. The Noh audience, trained in austere tastes, was a stable, unfluctuating element, and looked for a highly specialized and finished performance. The actors and playwrights enjoyed unprecedented social esteem, and the art was supported and protected by court patronage. This classical theater flourished in an enviable state of opulence. It was not the need for economy that led to the simplification of stage settings and stage production, though Yeats was not a little pleased with the inexpensiveness of the staging of his *Four Plays for Dancers*.

In the European theater tradition there is nothing as exclusive as the Noh. Though Greek drama was built around the lives of heroes, kings, and patricians, it was a seasonal, semireligious ritual for the whole populace. Shakespeare's plays were about both heroes and common men and were written and staged for Elizabethan courtiers and groundlings alike. Restoration comedy was exclusive and meant for a cavalier audience, but it was short-lived. Ibsen and Shaw and the early Yeats in their differing ways were by no means exclusive.

Therefore, in following the Japanese classical form Yeats was making a daring departure, both in regard to technique and in regard to audience.

The success of a dramatic work depends largely on the audience. A dramatist cannot entirely ignore contemporary popular tastes and values. In the present century a realistic approach is infinitely more agreeable to our factual, materialistic temper than any other approach. (The appeal of the theater of the absurd, for example, is strictly limited to the few who understand it.) A symbolic, visionary art is too select and restricted in its appeal, even though it can evoke a double response. A symbol can speak to our elemental, instinctive sense and it can appeal to a delicate spiritual sensibility or to the most sophisticated part of the mind. But to the average audience a symbol may present a barrier, whereas actually it is meant to suggest in an unconscious way personages, situations, and moods in all their complexity and fullness. The employment of private or scholarly or occult or even traditional symbolism can be baffling in a playhouse. The poetry of indirection, dream, myth, and free association, especially in the theater, is not everybody's fare. Nor is the Noh everybody's fare. If that is true in Japan, then how much more true is it outside Japan, where the style and experience of the Noh bear no relation to the already existing theater tradition?

The general lament concerning Yeat's dramatic innovations is that "the beautiful experiment of Mr. Yeats is doomed to have no posterity."[15] Cecil Day Lewis pays high tribute to the work of Yeats when he says: "No poet will be able to write after that manner again."[16] But does this matter? No one has been able to write like Shakespeare or Gerard Manley Hopkins or James Joyce. It is just as well that no one will be able to write like Yeats. His plays remain the rare gift of an auspicious moment in the history of the dramatic arts. Their permanence is assured whether there is a historical future for them or not. If one held the Oriental belief in reincarnation, one could visualize Yeats himself appearing again on the earthly scene, perhaps in India, or better still in Japan. Meanwhile, there will be plays, and plays for dancers, but no more Noble Plays for Dancers. In fact, it is doubtful that Yeats himself in his next birth would repeat the experiment. An artist of his restless curiosity would have moved on to still newer things.

Unfortunately, Yeats's Noh experiment is not left alone. Early critics found Yeats's experiment extravagant and farfetched. On the other hand, present-day critics are recommending possibilities of further experimentation along the lines of the Noh, from the point of view of non-Japanese audiences and productions. What is more, they are noticing Noh elements in both likely and unlikely places. There have been recent attempts in the West to write and produce plays in the Noh style, and also to reproduce the originals from Japan and the originals of Yeats. As far as the writing of plays goes, one might still succeed provided that one could master the rules of the craft and treat with some conviction subjects like family relationships, filial piety, ancestor worship, the ghost world, and myth and legend.

Henry W. Wells, in his book *The Classical Drama of the Orient,* sees Chinese and Japanese influences in Wallace Stevens's plays *Three Travellers Watch a Sunrise* and *Carlos Among the Candles* and in Kenneth Rexroth's *Beyond the Mountains.* These make good reading for contemplation, and contemplation is an integral function of the Noh. But the Noh is theater first and literature only secondarily. As a stage production a Noh play is magically transformed into a strange unfolding of possibilities not found in the meager text. This means that the magic of the Noh lies in great measure in the art of production and the imagination of the producer. For non-Japanese, matters of production pose severe difficulties. These difficulties have to do with a specialized kind of acting and actor, what the actors feel themselves, and what they make the playgoer feel. They have to do with music and dancing; with masks; with the stage setting and costumes required for a Noh production. The blending and perfection of these elements are the result of long discipline and patient craftsmanship. The only way in which such difficulties can be overcome is to modernize the Noh. Wells writes of a project he arranged for the production of nine Noh plays for a predominantly Negro college in the U.S.A. He found that Negro audiences responded more readily and sympathetically than European audiences to the theater of the East. But can one always isolate one's audience in this way? Wells admits that in such projects the Noh will undergo "fantastic changes" and that this will be "positively distasteful to the Japanese purist."

I am interested in the purist, and the Japanese purist, at that. Here much depends on one's philosophy of production. Should the Noh remain close to the original art or should it appeal to a wider audience both in and outside Japan? If we opt for the wider appeal, the Noh will undergo "fantastic changes" and lose its purity. If adaptations and changes in the Noh had been continuous from the time of its birth they would have become part and parcel of a growing process. Adaptations and changes introduced now into the long-finished product will not sit well on the old conventional art. The result will be a hybrid, false product, especially if non-Japanese are going to take the initiative. The Japanese purists, I know from personal experience, will not take such an initiative. They will continue to resist change in the Noh. For all their ultramodernity in practical life, the Japanese cultured minority are singularly conservative in aesthetic matters and jealously guard the traditions handed down to them by their forebears. They will not admit an uninitiated guest even as a distant spectator at a traditional tea ceremony. They have a great sense of reverence for such occasions. They have a penchant for the occult and cherish hints of a secret, select society.

Even Yeats's plays, which are not true Noh, have posed difficulties for producers both in Yeats's time and later. I shall take just one detail in later productions, stage settings and the use of masks, to illustrate this difficulty.

An article in *Bard Review* entitled "Stage Designs, Masks and Costumes for Plays of W. B. Yeats" by William Pitkin, with introductory notes by Sherman Conrad, includes sixteen sketches of stage sets, costumes, and masks for *At the Hawk's Well, The Only Jealousy of Emer,* and other plays—*The Player Queen, The Herne's Egg, The King of the Great Clock Tower,* and *A Full Moon in March.* William Pitkin, a gifted set designer confronted with problems of production, enunciates his own philosophy of production when he says: "I stress theatricality because these plays never make a pretense of reality and should never try. This is a theatre dream-world of color, voices, visions and imagination."[17] Pitkin's aim was theatricality as opposed to an illusion of reality.

By merely looking at the above-mentioned drawings I am in no position to form any but a tentative judgment. But the impression Pitkin's designs leave on the mind is that they would be excellent for some plays but do not blend well with the spirit of those of Yeats's plays that are constructed after the manner of the Noh. The costumes for the guardian of the well and the old man in *At the Hawk's Well,* and particularly those of the musicians, as well as the elaborate mask of Cuchulain, are far too spectacular and modern in tone for a "dream-world of color, voices, visions and imagination." The cloth for *At the Hawk's Well* is a masterpiece of artistic creation. It suggests a cosmic sweep and is extremely graceful. But everywhere there are obvious signs of studied workmanship. In the Japanese Noh costumes and masks the workmanship is equally studied and artful, but it gives the impression of being simple, retiring, and modest. The same objections hold for Pitkin's cloth for *The Only Jealousy of Emer.* I would feel distracted and stunned by such theatricality and the twentieth-century modernity in an art that is meant to have a visionary and interior quality. The masks and costumes designed by Yeats's contemporary artist-friends for the very first performances of these plays are equally modern, but considerably less startling than those of William Pitkin.

Revival of an ancient or traditional art even in the country of its birth is not easy. An Indian example comes to mind at this point. During the present cultural renaissance, many of India's arts and crafts, known as cottage industries, and much of our classical music and drama and other fine arts are being revived with great self-consciousness and gusto. The arts and crafts are doing very well for themselves both at home and abroad. But in the case of the fine arts the sponsorship of some of the very traditional and exclusive art forms is not encouraging.

Of these the classical Kathakali dance drama of South India readily suggests itself. For the Kathakali—with its half-mythical, half-human figures and demons, its spectacular, fustian costumes to enhance the heroic stature of the dancers, its masked players, its long ritual dances centered on a simple, abbreviated plot, its musical repertoire, and above all its symbolic representation—offers at first sight obvious parallels with the Noh theater of Japan. But I have chosen instead the Urdu *musha'ira* (poetry symposium), a nondramatic, intellectual art form, for illustration and comparison in preference to the Kathakali. For one thing, I am not familiar enough with the Kathakali dance drama to discuss its technicalities and fine points and advance a profitable critical opinion on it. Secondly, to my mind the Kathakali does not suggest the sophistication and overfastidiousness, the ceremony and quieter tempo that I find common to the atmosphere of the Noh drama and to the classical *musha'iras* of Persia and India, both in regard to their artistic qualities and spirit and in regard to their audiences and their sponsors. I must add without delay that what I am referring to here is decidedly not the present-day revival of the *musha'ira* with its mass, rambling, undisciplined audiences (I had almost said crowds), its glaring lights, and its amplified, raucous voices, but rather the quiet, leisurely, intimate *musha'ira* of, say, the good old days of Golconda and Bijapur, of Lucknow, Rampur, and Delhi, during the eighteenth and nineteenth centuries, at which noted poets of the day would grace the select occasion with their presence. These were primarily meetings of poets for poets.

I am thinking of something like the *musha'ira* described in Farhatulla Baig's charming little volume *Dehli ki Akhri Sham'a* ("The Last Lamp of Delhi," the lamp, *sham'a,* being a traditional symbol of a *musha'ira*). This half-historical, half-fictional *musha'ira* is supposed to have taken place at the Mughal court in the mid-nineteenth century under the auspices of Emperor Bahadur Shah Zafar, himself an accomplished poet, in a setting of exquisite sophistication, with the proper *musha'ira* decorum and formality, where noted poets of the day—Zauq, Momin, Ghalib, Shefta, Dagh—read their *ghazals,* written with the utmost conventionality and artifice, and where the delicate pleasure came as much from the *ghazal* poetry as from the voice of the reader. The stress laid upon the spoken word, the word listened to, is an additional point common to the Noh plays of Japan, Yeats's plays for dancers, and the *musha'ira*.

Because I am most familiar with Lucknow, I will take my examples chiefly from the Lucknow school favored by the *nawabs,* or rulers, of Oudh, notably Asif-ud-Daula and his son Wajid Ali Shah, both of the nineteenth century, under whom *musha'iras* celebrated the poetry of those luxurious, spacious times: the pleasures of nature and of love and friendship. These *musha'iras* were intellectual soirees at which renowned poets were invited to recite or sing their own works before a distinguished gathering of poetry lovers, themselves poets. The guests were well versed in classical Persian and Urdu: languages above all of refined emotions, subtle wit, paradox, irony, self-mockery, and elegance in social intercourse and polite speech.

The *musha'ira* would begin late in the evening after dinner and continue till dawn. There were no formalities of the modern kind, such as punctuality. Punctuality would have ruined the sense of leisure that was a marked feature of the occasion. But there were some traditional formalities. No women were present (at least they were not in sight; they might listen from behind a screen), though they were the subject of much of the *ghazal* poetry.

The poets came in formal dress. They leaned against white *gao-takiyas* (long bolsters) on thickly carpeted floors covered with the traditional white cloth. Each *ustad* (master) had his *baithak,* or seat, in the semicircular arrangement, where he and his *shagirds* (disciples) sat together. The host or patron poet sat in the center. The guests were served with *pan* and *supari* (betel leaf and betel nut) wrapped in superfine silver paper, and aromatic spices of the most delicate flavor, such as white *ilaichi* (cardamom), passed around on exquisitely carved silver trays. That was the utmost limit of hospitality. Food and drink were considered grossly mundane in a poetic context. Within the conventional format, the poets covered an amazing range of subjects—the secrets, infidelities, and transports of love; God, the abject sinner, the devotee longing for mystical union; death, time, youth, wine, and selfhood. The treatment of these themes was extremely individual and shot through with every subtlety of humor and every nuance of wisdom. In a half-serious, suavely bantering tone, the mockery often directed against himself, the poet would move his listeners to experiences of intellectual delight or emotional depth. In some cases hardly had the eye grown moist with sadness than the mind would begin to mock and toss about whatever there was to mock and toss about.

Musha'ira poetry, although it is a poetry of solitude, the poet for the most part communing with himself, was created for the listener, not necessarily for the reader. Without the listener there could be no *musha'ira*. The poet and the trained listener would establish an immediate rapport not possible on other occasions. In the recitation every single word was given its proper place and weight. The economy was so severe that not a syllable could be missed without imparing the meaning and the enjoyment of the line. In the intimacy of the enchanted circle, the poet knew from the audience response when to repeat, as many as three or four times, a fastidiously worded line or an extra felicitous phrase. With bated breath the audience waited for the last words of the lines containing the pith and point of the couplet or some unforeseen twist of thought. Often the recitation of the *ghazal* was interrupted by spontaneous applause in words like "*Subhan Allah, subhan Allah*" (God be praised) or "*Marhaba*" (Bravo), and cries of "*Muqarrar irshad, muqarrar irshad*" (Encore). Altogether, the poet would throw the group into a mood of rapt intoxication. I have known this mood, though extremely rarely, even at modest *musha'ira* gatherings, where the courtly element was absent, no doubt, but where the listener and the poet still retained the love of poetry and respected and preserved the conventions and atmosphere of the original entertainment.

Musha'iras in Lucknow were sponsored by the *nawabs* of Oudh and the affluent *taluqdari* class, the landed gentry. They were the only patrons of the fine arts in Oudh at that time and treated the scholar, the poet, the musician, the painter, and the illuminator of books with a fine and free generosity. Not a few spent their hereditary wealth to beautify cities, to build mosques and *imambaras* (cenotaphs of the *imams,* spiritual leaders of the Shiyya sect of Islam), and to lay out public parks and gardens. Their splendid capacity for pleasure and idleness and their aristocratic tastes imparted a special quality to their manner of life. In some respects they were very much like the Japanese Noh patrons, but with a difference. The difference, I suppose, came from their being Indian and Muslim and courtly, instead of members of the strenuous martial aristocracy of feudal Japan.

Lacking the leisure and spirit of an aristocratic and self-conscious culture and the listener with a knowledge of Urdu and Persian, the authentic note is bound to be missing in the *musha'ira* today. Although I am not fortunate enough to have been present at the original *musha'iras* of the Bijapur and Hyderabad or the Delhi and Lucknow schools as they flourished over the centuries, I feel that I know in some mysterious way what the originals must have been like. The Japanese, likewise, know that modern Noh does not do justice to the original. It would seem as impossible to produce a replica of the truly traditional *musha'ira* in modern India as it is to produce the authentic Noh in modern Japan. Some undefinable element will always be absent.

I think the Noh would suffer greater damage in the process of adaptation and change than the *musha'ira* because the Noh is the more elaborate and the more highly stylized and ritualistic an art. I shall not be dogmatic about this, nor do my conclusions refer to all the classical arts. If neither the authentic art nor the proper milieu and audience can be created, I wonder if it is not wisest to accept the limited appeal of some classical art and to keep inviolate at least its "classicness" or its "ancientness." However universal the experiences they portray, I can reach Shakespeare or the great Persian Sufi poet Firdausi only if I know the respective languages in which their works were written. A fairly long and arduous discipline must precede the enjoyment of the Noh or the *musha'ira* or Shakespeare or Firdausi. The failure of Yeats's dramatic experiment was due to the absence of more basic factors than technical discipline—that is, the absence of centuries of tradition, both social and artistic.

I suggest one other consideration. It seems to me that the attempts in the West to modernize the Noh betray ulterior motives—very sublime ulterior motives, I hasten to add—such as good international relations through synthesis and integration of cultures, especially between those of the East and the West, and more especially between those of Japan and the U.S.A. Japan has been particularly insular, and good neighbors would like to see a breakthrough of the isolation at deeper levels than those of industrialization, trade, commerce, and political alliances. This is desirable. But I think it is more desirable, more realistic, and more helpful to express our good will and international sense first on the political, economic, and technological fronts. In the modern world it is expressions of religion and culture and the fine arts that make societies distinct from one another and for that reason interesting and attractive. We might preserve this lure for one another in a civilization that is rapidly becoming homogeneous and coldly standardized.

Last, I hazard one further observation, although I do so with extreme diffidence.

Contemporary Western civilization produces and honors men of action, men of progressive and adventurous ideas. Men of contemplation have a small place not only in the West but increasingly in the East also. In addition, the Western temperament and intellectual makeup are too vigorous, too impatient, too restless, too conscious of time passing for as quiet and static an art as the Noh or any drama modeled on it. From the time of Ulysses to contemporary space explorers, scientists, and technicians, Western civilization has prospered on conflict, high endeavor, curiosity, the kick and thrust of action: qualities we in the East do not come by naturally but are trying to cultivate in order to take our place in the competitive world of today. I am not sure that I do not half regret this our modern ambition. The vigorous, active West, on the other hand, has fitfully and sometimes romantically, sometimes seriously, searched for the fabled Eastern repose, unity of being, and transcendence. (The last expedition along these lines lacked all the high motivation and fine attitudes of attempts in earlier centuries and was a brief one. The hippies no sooner embraced than they abandoned the search, either because they were disenchanted with Indian transcendentalism or with its particular expression in the contemporary Rishikesh school, or because it was too difficult a discipline for a generation brought up on things made easy.)

Even to us in the Orient the great *rishis* of the Upanishad period, the Sufis of Persia, and the Zen Buddhists of China and Japan seem remote and mythical. They were once real and I believe such people still exist in favored spots around the world. To put it baldly and perhaps invite upon myself the charge of conservatism or of heresy in this democratic and in many ways synthetic age, the emotional and intellectual climate suited to certain highly specialized and contemplative or leisurely arts, for reasons implied throughout this work, is nonexistent in our time. Such arts are often created by minority taste and sponsorship, but for which they would never come into being (the term "minority" can refer equally to the less aristocratic, less opulent folk minority as to the nobility).

The Noh plays of Japan and Yeats's plays for dancers are brilliant spots of eccentricity in theater. They are meant for an eccentric minority taste nourished and shaped by a certain tradition, outlook, and cultural atmosphere. If and when they are revived for modern audiences, they should suffer no violent alteration, in fact no alteration at all in their traditional dramatic technique and mood. In short, they should be played before a secret society "where admission is by favour and never to many."

NOTES TO THE TEXT

PREFACE

1. W. B. Yeats, *A Vision*, p. 279.

One: YEATS AND
THE SYMBOLISTS

1. Arthur Symons, *The Symbolist Movement in Literature*, p. v.
2. W. B. Yeats, *Mythologies*, p. 367.
3. William York Tindall, *Forces in Modern British Literature: 1885–1946*, p. 254.
4. Ibid., p. 250.
5. Yeats, *Essays*, p. 33.
6. Yeats, *Autobiographies*, p. 109.
7. Stanley Edgar Hymen, *Armed Vision*, p. 347.
8. Plotinus, *The Six Enneads*, trans. Stephen MacKenna and B. S. Page, pp. 239–40.
9. C. S. Lewis, *English Literature in the Sixteenth Century*, p. 320.
10. Désirée Hirst, *Hidden Riches*, p. 24.
11. Ibid., pp. 309–10.
12. Margaret Rudd, *Divided Image*, pp. 186–87.
13. Yeats, *A Vision*, p. 13.

Two: IRISH THEATER:
THE GOLDEN BRIDGE

1. William York Tindall, *Forces in Modern British Literature: 1885–1946*, p. 78.
2. C. H. Herford, "The Scandinavian Dramatists 1840–1860," p. 14.
3. Richard Ellmann, *Yeats: The Man and the Masks*, p. 99.
4. W. B. Yeats, *Autobiographies*, p. 396.
5. Gerard Murphy, "Douglas Hyde," p. 278.
6. Yeats, *Autobiographies*, p. 396.
7. Yeats, *Explorations*, p. 74.
8. Yeats, *Four Plays for Dancers*, p. 86.
9. Una Ellis-Fermor, *The Irish Dramatic Movement*, p. 211.
10. Emile Legouis and Louis Cazamian, *A History of English Literature*, pp. 1,321–22.
11. Yeats, Preface, *Cuchulain of Muirthemne* by Augusta Gregory, p. xiii.
12. Legouis and Cazamian, *English Literature*, p. 1,321.
13. Yeats, *Explorations*, p. 166.
14. Ibid., p. 167.
15. Ibid., p. 198.
16. Edward Martyn, "Comparison Between English and Irish Theatrical Audience," *Beltaine*.
17. George Moore, "Is the Theatre a

115

Place for Amusement?" *Beltaine.*
18. Yeats, *Explorations,* p. 111.
19. Ibid., p. 116.
20. Gerard Fay, "The Abbey Theatre," p. 28.
21. Yeats, *Explorations,* p. 176.
22. Ibid., p. 173.
23. Clifford Bax, ed., *Florence Farr, Bernard Shaw, W. B. Yeats: Letters,* p. v.
24. Yeats, *Explorations,* pp. 107–20 passim.
25. Yeats, *Autobiographies,* p. 435.
26. Yeats, *Explorations,* pp. 148, 151.
27. Ibid., p. 156.
28. Ibid., p. 94.
29. Ibid., p. 81.
30. Yeats, *Autobiographies,* p. 396.
31. Yeats, *Explorations,* pp. 86–87.
32. Ibid., pp. 109–10.
33. Ibid.

Three: YEATS AND THE
NOH PLAYS OF JAPAN

1. James Joyce, "A Letter from Mr. Joyce to the Publisher," *Ulysses* (New York: Modern Library, Random House, 1934), p. xvi.
2. Richard Ellmann, *Yeats: The Man and the Masks,* p. 211.
3. Ibid., p. 212.
4. W. B. Yeats, *Plays and Controversies,* p. 214.
5. Ellmann, *Yeats,* pp. 212–13.
6. Ibid., p. 214.
7. Gerard Fay, "The Abbey Theatre," p. 30.
8. W. G. Fay, "The Poet and the Actor," *Scattering Branches,* ed. Stephen Gwynn, p. 132.
9. Some of the following material on

Japanese aesthetics is adapted from a talk I gave on All India Radio, and is included here with the permission of A.I.R.
10. Ernest Fenollosa and Ezra Pound, *'Noh' or Accomplishment: A Study of the Classical Stage of Japan,* p. 4.
11. Ezra Pound and Ernest Fenollosa, *The Classic Noh Theatre of Japan,* p. 64.
12. Zeami Motokiyo, *Birds of Sorrow,* translation of the Noh play *Uto* by Meredith Weatherby and Bruce Rogers, pp. 29, 64.
13. Japanese Classics Translation Committee, *The Noh Drama,* p. 14.
14. Fenollosa and Pound, *'Noh' or Accomplishment,* p. 27.

Four: YEATS AND THE
PLAYS FOR DANCERS

1. W. B. Yeats, "Note on the First Performance of 'At the Hawk's Well,' " *Four Plays for Dancers,* p. 86.
2. Yeats, "Introduction by William Butler Yeats," *The Classic Noh Theatre of Japan* by Ezra Pound and Ernest Fenollosa, p. 151.
3. Yeats, *The Cutting of an Agate,* p. v.
4. Pound and Fenollosa, *The Classic Noh Theatre,* p. 104.
5. Yeats, *Explorations,* p. 51.
6. Yeats, "Note on the First Performance of 'At the Hawk's Well,' " *Four Plays for Dancers,* p. 86.
7. Yeats, *Explorations,* p. 256.
8. Yeats, *Four Plays for Dancers,* p. **vi.**
9. Ibid., p. vii.
10. Yeats, "Introduction," *The Classic*

Noh Theatre by Pound and Fenollosa, p. 155.

11. Yeats, "Note on the First Performance of 'At the Hawk's Well,' " *Four Plays for Dancers,* pp. 86–87.
12. Yeats, *Four Plays for Dancers,* p. v.
13. Ibid.
14. Yeats, "Introduction," *The Classic Noh Theatre,* p. 154.
15. Yeats, "Note on 'Calvary,' " *Four Plays for Dancers,* p. 136.

Five: THE SPLENDOR AND SORROWS OF THE RED BRANCH

1. W. B. Yeats, Preface, *Cuchulain of Muirthemne* by Augusta Gregory, p. vii.
2. Ibid., p. iv.
3. Ibid., p. v.
4. Yeats, *Dramatis Personae,* p. 79.
5. Richard Ellmann, *Yeats: The Man and the Masks,* pp. 7–10.
6. Yeats, *Autobiographies,* p. 6.
7. Ibid., p. 83.
8. Ibid., p. 7.
9. Ibid., p. 9.
10. Yeats, *Mythologies,* p. 56.
11. Yeats, ed., *Irish Folk Stories and Fairy Tales,* p. xiii.
12. Augusta Gregory, *Cuchulain of Muirthemne,* p. 1.
13. Ibid., p. 2.
14. Ibid., p. 67.
15. Ibid., p. 57.
16. Ibid., p. 60.
17. Ibid., p. 61.
18. Yeats, "Note on the First Performance of 'At the Hawk's Well,' " *Four Plays for Dancers,* pp. 87–88.
19. Lennox Robinson, "The Man and

the Dramatist," *Scattering Branches,* ed. Stephen Gwynn, p. 108.
20. All quotations from Yeats's plays, except where otherwise noted, are from the versions in *Collected Plays of W. B. Yeats.*
21. Peter Ure, *Yeats the Playwright,* p. 71.
22. Walter Morse Rummel, "Music for 'The Dreaming of the Bones,' " *Four Plays for Dancers* by Yeats, p. 108.
23. Gregory, *Cuchulain of Muirthemne,* p. 277.
24. Yeats, *Four Plays for Dancers,* p. 45.
25. Ibid., p. 46.
26. Yeats, Preface, *Four Plays for Dancers,* p. vi.
27. Yeats, *Autobiographies,* p. 152.
28. Yeats, "Note on 'The Only Jealousy of Emer,' " *Four Plays for Dancers,* p. 105.
29. Ibid., p. 106.
30. Yeats, "The Trembling of the Veil," pp. 447–48.

Six: EVALUATION

1. Louis MacNeice, *The Poetry of W. B. Yeats,* pp. 187–89.
2. Ibid., pp. 188–89.
3. O. W. Firkins, " 'Four Plays for Dancers' by W. B. Yeats," p. 196.
4. Edmund Wilson, "The Poetry of W. B. Yeats."
5. Lennox Robinson, "The Man and the Dramatist," *Scattering Branches,* ed. Stephen Gwynn, pp. 107–8.
6. L. A. G. Strong, "W. B. Yeats," *Scattering Branches,* pp. 222–27.
7. "The Wizardry of Mr. Yeats:

'Four Plays for Dancers,' " p. 643.

8. " 'Four Plays for Dancers' by Yeats," p. 840.

9. W. B. Yeats, *Explorations*, pp. 244–57 passim.

10. Yeats, Preface, *Cuchulain of Muirthemne* by Augusta Gregory, p. xv.

11. Ezra Pound and Ernest Fenollosa, *The Classic Noh Theatre of Japan*, p. 152.

12. Yeats, *A Vision*, pp. 279–80.

13. Yeats, "Note on 'The Only Jealousy of Emer,' " *Four Plays for Dancers*, p. 106.

14. Pound and Fenollosa, *The Classic Noh Theatre*, p. 155.

15. "The Wizardry of Mr. Yeats," p. 643.

16. Cecil Day Lewis, "A Note on W. B. Yeats and the Aristocratic Tradition," *Scattering Branches*, p. 159.

17. William Pitkin, "Stage Designs, Masks and Costumes for Plays of W. B. Yeats," p. 94.

APPENDIX: FOUR PLAYS

W. B. Yeats   AT THE HAWK'S WELL

PERSONS IN THE PLAY

Three Musicians (*their faces made up to resemble masks*)
The Guardian of the Well (*with face made up to resemble a mask*)
An Old Man (*wearing a mask*)
A Young Man (*wearing a mask*)

Time—the Irish Heroic Age

The stage is any bare space before a wall against which stands a patterned screen. A drum and a gong and a zither have been laid close to the screen before the play begins. If necessary, they can be carried in, after the audience is seated, by the First Musician, who also can attend to the lights if there is any special lighting. We had two lanterns upon posts—designed by Mr. Dulac—at the outer corners of the stage, but they did not give enough light, and we found it better to play by the light of a large chandelier. Indeed, I think, so far as my present experience goes, that the most effective lighting is the lighting we are most accustomed to in our rooms. These masked players seem stranger when there is no mechanical means of separating them from us. The First Musician carries with him a folded black cloth and goes to the centre of the stage towards the front and stands motionless, the folded cloth hanging from between his hands. The two other Musicians enter and, after standing a moment at either side of the stage, go towards him and slowly unfold the cloth, singing as they do so:

> I call to the eye of the mind
> A well long choked up and dry
> And boughs long stripped by the wind,
> And I call to the mind's eye

> Pallor of an ivory face,
> Its lofty dissolute air,
> A man climbing up to a place
> The salt sea wind has swept bare.

As they unfold the cloth, they go backward a little so that the stretched cloth and the wall make a triangle with the First Musician at the apex supporting the centre of the cloth. On the black cloth is a gold pattern suggesting a hawk. The Second and Third Musicians now slowly fold up the cloth again, pacing with a rhythmic movement of the arms towards the First Musician and singing:

> What were his life soon done!
> Would he lose by that or win?
> A mother that saw her son
> Doubled over a speckled shin,
> Cross-grained with ninety years,
> Would cry, 'How little worth
> Were all my hopes and fears
> And the hard pain of his birth!'

The words 'a speckled shin' are familiar to readers of Irish legendary stories in descriptions of old men bent double over the fire. While the cloth has been spread out, the Guardian of the Well has entered and is now crouching upon the ground. She is entirely covered by a black cloak; beside her lies a square blue cloth to represent a well. The three Musicians have taken their places against the wall beside their instruments of music; they will accompany the movements of the players with gong or drum or zither.

FIRST MUSICIAN [*singing*].
> The boughs of the hazel shake,
> The sun goes down in the west.

SECOND MUSICIAN [*singing*].
> The heart would be always awake,
> The heart would turn to its rest.

> [*They now go to one side of the stage rolling up the cloth.*]

FIRST MUSICIAN [*speaking*].   Night falls;
> The mountain-side grows dark;
> The withered leaves of the hazel
> Half choke the dry bed of the well;
> The guardian of the well is sitting
> Upon the old grey stone at its side,

Worn out from raking its dry bed,
Worn out from gathering up the leaves.
Her heavy eyes
Know nothing, or but look upon stone.
The wind that blows out of the sea
Turns over the heaped-up leaves at her side;
They rustle and diminish.

SECOND MUSICIAN.   I am afraid of this place.

BOTH MUSICIANS [*singing*].

> 'Why should I sleep?' the heart cries,
> 'For the wind, the salt wind, the sea wind,
> Is beating a cloud through the skies;
> I would wander always like the wind.'

> > > [*An Old Man enters through the audience.*]

FIRST MUSICIAN [*speaking*].   That old man climbs up hither,
Who has been watching by his well
These fifty years.
He is all doubled up with age;
The old thorn-trees are doubled so
Among the rocks where he is climbing.

[*The Old Man stands for a moment motionless by the side of the stage with bowed head. He lifts his head at the sound of a drum-tap. He goes towards the front of the stage moving to the taps of the drum. He crouches and moves his hands as if making a fire. His movements, like those of the other persons of the play, suggest a marionette*].

FIRST MUSICIAN [*speaking*].   He has made a little heap of leaves;
He lays the dry sticks on the leaves
And, shivering with cold, he has taken up
The fire-stick and socket from its hole.
He whirls it round to get a flame;
And now the dry sticks take the fire,
And now the fire leaps up and shines
Upon the hazels and the empty well.

MUSICIANS [*singing*].

> 'O wind, O salt wind, O sea wind!'
> Cries the heart, 'it is time to sleep;
> Why wander and nothing to find?
> Better grow old and sleep.'

OLD MAN [*speaking*].   Why don't you speak to me? Why don't you say:

'Are you not weary gathering those sticks?
Are not your fingers cold?' You have not one word,
While yesterday you spoke three times. You said:
'The well is full of hazel leaves.' You said:
'The wind is from the west.' And after that:
'If there is rain it's likely there'll be mud.'
To-day you are as stupid as a fish,
No, worse, worse, being less lively and as dumb.

> [*He goes nearer.*]

Your eyes are dazed and heavy. If the Sidhe
Must have a guardian to clean out the well
And drive the cattle off, they might choose somebody
That can be pleasant and companionable
Once in the day. Why do you stare like that?
You had that glassy look about the eyes
Last time it happened. Do you know anything?
It is enough to drive an old man crazy
To look all day upon these broken rocks,
And ragged thorns, and that one stupid face,
And speak and get no answer.

YOUNG MAN [*who has entered through the audience during the last speech*].
Then speak to me,
For youth is not more patient than old age;
And though I have trod the rocks for half a day
I cannot find what I am looking for.

OLD MAN.   Who speaks?
Who comes so suddenly into this place
Where nothing thrives? If I may judge by the gold
On head and feet and glittering in your coat,
You are not of those who hate the living world.

YOUNG MAN.   I am named Cuchulain, I am Sualtim's son.

OLD MAN.   I have never heard that name.

YOUNG MAN.   It is not unknown.
I have an ancient house beyond the sea.

OLD MAN.   What mischief brings you hither?—you are like those
Who are crazy for the shedding of men's blood,
And for the love of women.

YOUNG MAN.   A rumour has led me,
A story told over the wine towards dawn.

I rose from table, found a boat, spread sail,
And with a lucky wind under the sail
Crossed waves that have seemed charmed, and found this shore.

OLD MAN.   There is no house to sack among these hills
Nor beautiful woman to be carried off.

YOUNG MAN.   You should be native here, for that rough tongue
Matches the barbarous spot. You can, it may be,
Lead me to what I seek, a well wherein
Three hazels drop their nuts and withered leaves,
And where a solitary girl keeps watch
Among grey boulders. He who drinks, they say,
Of that miraculous water lives for ever.

OLD MAN.   And are there not before your eyes at the instant
Grey boulders and a solitary girl
And three stripped hazels?

YOUNG MAN.   But there is no well.

OLD MAN.   Can you see nothing yonder?

YOUNG MAN.   I but see
A hollow among stones half-full of leaves.

OLD MAN.   And do you think so great a gift is found
By no more toil than spreading out a sail,
And climbing a steep hill? O, folly of youth,
Why should that hollow place fill up for you,
That will not fill for me? I have lain in wait
For more than fifty years, to find it empty,
Or but to find the stupid wind of the sea
Drive round the perishable leaves.

YOUNG MAN.   So it seems
There is some moment when the water fills it.

OLD MAN.   A secret moment that the holy shades
That dance upon the desolate mountain know,
And not a living man, and when it comes
The water has scarce plashed before it is gone.

YOUNG MAN.   I will stand here and wait. Why should the luck
Of Sualtim's son desert him now? For never
Have I had long to wait for anything.

OLD MAN.   No! Go from this accursed place! This place
Belongs to me, that girl there, and those others,
Deceivers of men.

YOUNG MAN.   And who are you who rail
   Upon those dancers that all others bless?
OLD MAN.   One whom the dancers cheat. I came like you
   When young in body and in mind, and blown
   By what had seemed to me a lucky sail.
   The well was dry, I sat upon its edge,
   I waited the miraculous flood, I waited
   While the years passed and withered me away.
   I have snared the birds for food and eaten grass
   And drunk the rain, and neither in dark nor shine
   Wandered too far away to have heard the plash,
   And yet the dancers have deceived me. Thrice
   I have awakened from a sudden sleep
   To find the stones were wet.
YOUNG MAN.   My luck is strong,
   It will not leave me waiting, nor will they
   That dance among the stones put me asleep;
   If I grow drowsy I can pierce my foot.
OLD MAN.   No, do not pierce it, for the foot is tender,
   It feels pain much. But find your sail again
   And leave the well to me, for it belongs
   To all that's old and withered.
YOUNG MAN.   No, I stay.
            [*The Guardian of the Well gives the cry of the hawk.*]
   There is that bird again.
OLD MAN.   There is no bird.
YOUNG MAN.   It sounded like the sudden cry of a hawk,
   But there's no wing in sight. As I came hither
   A great grey hawk swept down out of the sky,
   And though I have good hawks, the best in the world
   I had fancied, I have not seen its like. It flew
   As though it would have torn me with its beak,
   Or blinded me, smiting with that great wing.
   I had to draw my sword to drive it off,
   And after that it flew from rock to rock.
   I pelted it with stones, a good half-hour,
   And just before I had turned the big rock there
   And seen this place, it seemed to vanish away.

Could I but find a means to bring it down
I'd hood it.

OLD MAN.   The Woman of the Sidhe herself,
The mountain witch, the unappeasable shadow.
She is always flitting upon this mountain-side,
To allure or to destroy. When she has shown
Herself to the fierce women of the hills
Under that shape they offer sacrifice
And arm for battle. There falls a curse
On all who have gazed in her unmoistened eyes;
So get you gone while you have that proud step
And confident voice, for not a man alive
Has so much luck that he can play with it.
Those that have long to live should fear her most,
The old are cursed already. That curse may be
Never to win a woman's love and keep it;
Or always to mix hatred in the love;
Or it may be that she will kill your children,
That you will find them, their throats torn and bloody,
Or you will be so maddened that you kill them
With your own hand.

YOUNG MAN.   Have you been set down there
To threaten all who come, and scare them off?
You seem as dried up as the leaves and sticks,
As though you had no part in life.

                    [*The Guardian of the Well gives hawk cry again.*]
                         That cry!
There is that cry again. That woman made it,
But why does she cry out as the hawk cries?

OLD MAN. It was her mouth, and yet not she, that cried.
It was that shadow cried behind her mouth;
And now I know why she has been so stupid
All the day through, and had such heavy eyes.
Look at her shivering now, the terrible life
Is slipping through her veins. She is possessed.
Who knows whom she will murder or betray
Before she awakes in ignorance of it all,
And gathers up the leaves? But they'll be wet;

The water will have come and gone again;
That shivering is the sign. O, get you gone,
At any moment now I shall hear it bubble.
If you are good you will leave it. I am old,
And if I do not drink it now, will never;
I have been watching all my life and maybe
Only a little cupful will bubble up.

YOUNG MAN.   I'll take it in my hands. We shall both drink,
And even if there are but a few drops,
Share them.

OLD MAN.   But swear that I may drink the first;
The young are greedy, and if you drink the first
You'll drink it all. Ah, you have looked at her;
She has felt your gaze and turned her eyes on us;
I cannot bear her eyes, they are not of this world,
Nor moist, nor faltering; they are no girl's eyes.

[*He covers his head. The Guardian of the Well throws off her cloak and rises. Her dress under the cloak suggests a hawk.*]

YOUNG MAN.   Why do you fix those eyes of a hawk upon me?
I am not afraid of you, bird, woman, or witch.

[*He goes to the side of the well, which the Guardian of the Well has left.*]
Do what you will, I shall not leave this place
Till I have grown immortal like yourself.

[*He has sat down; the Guardian of the Well has begun to dance, moving like a hawk. The Old Man sleeps. The dance goes on for some time.*]

FIRST MUSICIAN [*singing or half-singing*].
                    O God, protect me
                    From a horrible deathless body
                    Sliding through the veins of a sudden.

[*The dance goes on for some time. The Young Man rises slowly.*]

FIRST MUSICIAN [*speaking*].   The madness has laid hold upon him now,
For he grows pale and staggers to his feet.

[*The dance goes on.*]

YOUNG MAN.   Run where you will,
Grey bird, you shall be perched upon my wrist.
Some were called queens and yet have been perched there.

[*The dance goes on.*]

FIRST MUSICIAN [*speaking*].   I have heard water plash; it comes, it comes;

Look where it glitters. He has heard the plash;
Look, he has turned his head.

[*The Guardian of the Well has gone out. The Young Man drops his spear as if in a dream and goes out.*]

MUSICIANS [*singing*].

> He has lost what may not be found
> Till men heap his burial-mound
> And all the history ends.
> He might have lived at his ease,
> An old dog's head on his knees,
> Among his children and friends.

[*The Old Man creeps up to the well.*]

OLD MAN.   The accursed shadows have deluded me,
The stones are dark and yet the well is empty;
The water flowed and emptied while I slept.
You have deluded me my whole life through,
Accursed dancers, you have stolen my life.
That there should be such evil in a shadow!

YOUNG MAN [*entering*].   She has fled from me and hidden in the rocks.

OLD MAN.   She has but led you from the fountain. Look!
Though stones and leaves are dark where it has flowed,
There's not a drop to drink.

[*The Musicians cry 'Aoife!' 'Aoife!' and strike gong.*]

YOUNG MAN.   What are those cries?
What is that sound that runs along the hill?
Who are they that beat a sword upon a shield?

OLD MAN.   She has roused up the fierce women of the hills,
Aoife, and all her troop, to take your life,
And never till you are lying in the earth
Can you know rest.

YOUNG MAN.   The clash of arms again!

OLD MAN.   O, do not go! The mountain is accursed;
Stay with me, I have nothing more to lose,
I do not now deceive you.

YOUNG MAN.   I will face them.

[*He goes out, no longer as if in a dream, but shouldering his spear and calling:*]
He comes! Cuchulain, son of Sualtim, comes!

[*The Musicians stand up; one goes to centre with folded cloth. The others unfold it. While they do so they sing. During the singing, and while hidden by the cloth, the Old Man goes out. When the play is performed with Mr. Dulac's music, the Musicians do not rise or unfold the cloth till after they have sung the words 'a bitter life'.]*

[*Songs for the unfolding and folding of the cloth*]

Come to me, human faces,
Familiar memories;
I have found hateful eyes
Among the desolate places,
Unfaltering, unmoistened eyes.

Folly alone I cherish,
I choose it for my share;
Being but a mouthful of air,
I am content to perish;
I am but a mouthful of sweet air.

O lamentable shadows,
Obscurity of strife!
I choose a pleasant life
Among indolent meadows;
Wisdom must live a bitter life.

[*They then fold up the cloth, singing.*]

'The man that I praise',
Cries out the empty well,
'Lives all his days
Where a hand on the bell
Can call the milch cows
To the comfortable door of his house.
Who but an idiot would praise
Dry stones in a well?'

'The man that I praise',
Cries out the leafless tree,
'Has married and stays
By an old hearth, and he
On naught has set store
But children and dogs on the floor.
Who but an idiot would praise
A withered tree?'   [*They go out.*]

W. B. Yeats   THE DREAMING OF THE BONES

PERSONS IN THE PLAY

Three Musicians (*their faces made up to resemble masks*)
A Young Man
A Stranger (*wearing a mask*)
A Young Girl (*wearing a mask*)

Time—1916

The stage is any bare place in a room close to the wall. A screen, with a pattern of mountain and sky, can stand against the wall, or a curtain with a like pattern hang upon it, but the pattern must only symbolise or suggest. One Musician enters and then two others; the first stands singing, as in preceding plays, while the others take their places. Then all three sit down against the wall by their instruments, which are already there—a drum, a zither, and a flute. Or they unfold a cloth as in 'At the Hawk's Well', while the instruments are carried in.

[*Song for the folding and unfolding of the cloth*]

FIRST MUSICIAN [*or all three Musicians, singing*].

   Why does my heart beat so?
   Did not a shadow pass?
   It passed but a moment ago.
   Who can have trod in the grass?
   What rogue is night-wandering?
   Have not old writers said
   That dizzy dreams can spring
   From the dry bones of the dead?
   And many a night it seems

That all the valley fills
With those fantastic dreams.
They overflow the hills,
So passionate is a shade,
Like wine that fills to the top
A grey-green cup of jade,
Or maybe an agate cup.

[*The three Musicians are now seated by the drum, flute, and zither at the back of the stage. The First Musician speaks.*]

The hour before dawn and the moon covered up;
The little village of Abbey is covered up;
The little narrow trodden way that runs
From the white road to the Abbey of Corcomroe
Is covered up; and all about the hills
Are like a circle of agate or of jade.
Somewhere among great rocks on the scarce grass
Birds cry, they cry their loneliness.
Even the sunlight can be lonely here,
Even hot noon is lonely. I hear a footfall—
A young man with a lantern comes this way.
He seems an Aran fisher, for he wears
The flannel bawneen and the cow-hide shoe.
He stumbles wearily, and stumbling prays.

[*A Young Man enters, praying in Irish.*]

Once more the birds cry in their loneliness,
But now they wheel about our heads; and now
They have dropped on the grey stone to the northeast.

[*A Stranger and a Young Girl, in the costume of a past time, come in. They wear heroic masks.*]

YOUNG MAN [*raising his lantern*]. Who is there? I cannot see what you
        are like.
    Come to the light.

STRANGER.   But what have you to fear?

YOUNG MAN.   And why have you come creeping through the dark?

[*The Girl blows out lantern.*]

The wind has blown my lantern out. Where are you?
I saw a pair of heads against the sky
And lost them after; but you are in the right,
I should not be afraid in County Clare;

And should be, or should not be, have no choice,
I have to put myself into your hands,
Now that my candle's out.

STRANGER. You have fought in Dublin?

YOUNG MAN. I was in the Post Office, and if taken
I shall be put against a wall and shot.

STRANGER. You know some place of refuge, have some plan
Or friend who will come to meet you?

YOUNG MAN. I am to lie
At daybreak on the mountain and keep watch
Until an Aran coracle puts in
At Muckanish or at the rocky shore
Under Finvara, but would break my neck
If I went stumbling there alone in the dark.

STRANGER. We know the pathways that the sheep tread out,
And all the hiding-places of the hills,
And that they had better hiding-places once.

YOUNG MAN. You'd say they had better before English robbers
Cut down the trees or set them upon fire
For fear their owners might find shelter there.
What is that sound?

STRANGER. An old horse gone astray.
He has been wandering on the road all night.

YOUNG MAN. I took him for a man and horse. Police
Are out upon the roads. In the late Rising
I think there was no man of us but hated
To fire at soldiers who but did their duty
And were not of our race, but when a man
Is born in Ireland and of Irish stock,
When he takes part against us—

STRANGER. I will put you safe,
No living man shall set his eyes upon you;
I will not answer for the dead.

YOUNG MAN. The dead?

STRANGER. For certain days the stones where you must lie
Have in the hour before the break of day
Been haunted.

YOUNG MAN. But I was not born at midnight.

STRANGER. Many a man that was born in the full daylight

Can see them plain, will pass them on the high-road
Or in the crowded market-place of the town,
And never know that they have passed.

YOUNG MAN. My Grandam
Would have it they did penance everywhere;
Some lived through their old lives again.

STRANGER. In a dream;
And some for an old scruple must hang spitted
Upon the swaying tops of lofty trees;
Some are consumed in fire, some withered up
By hail and sleet out of the wintry North,
And some but live through their old lives again.

YOUNG MAN. Well, let them dream into what shape they please
And fill waste mountains with the invisible tumult
Of the fantastic conscience. I have no dread;
They cannot put me into gaol or shoot me;
And seeing that their blood has returned to fields
That have grown red from drinking blood like mine,
They would not if they could betray.

STRANGER. This pathway
Runs to the ruined Abbey of Corcomroe;
The Abbey passed, we are soon among the stone
And shall be at the ridge before the cocks
Of Aughanish or Bailevelehan
Or grey Aughtmana shake their wings and cry.

[*They go round the stage once.*]

FIRST MUSICIAN [*speaking*]. They've passed the shallow well and the flat stone
Fouled by the drinking cattle, the narrow lane
Where mourners for five centuries have carried
Noble or peasant to his burial;
An owl is crying out above their heads.

[*Singing*]
Why should the heart take fright?
What sets it beating so?
The bitter sweetness of the night
Has made it but a lonely thing.
Red bird of March, begin to crow!
Up with the neck and clap the wing,
Red cock, and crow!

[*They go round the stage once. The First Musician speaks.*]
And now they have climbed through the long grassy field
And passed the ragged thorn-trees and the gap
In the ancient hedge; and the tomb-nested owl
At the foot's level beats with a vague wing.

[*Singing*]
My head is in a cloud;
I'd let the whole world go;
My rascal heart is proud
Remembering and remembering.
Red bird of March, begin to crow!
Up with the neck and clap the wing,
Red cock, and crow!

[*They go round the stage once. The First Musician speaks.*]
They are among the stones above the ash,
Above the briar and thorn and the scarce grass;
Hidden amid the shadow far below them
The cat-headed bird is crying out.

[*Singing*]
The dreaming bones cry out
Because the night winds blow
And heaven's a cloudy blot.
Calamity can have its fling.
Red bird of March, begin to crow!
Up with the neck and clap the wing,
Red cock, and crow!

STRANGER.   We're almost at the summit and can rest.
The road is a faint shadow there; and there
The Abbey lies amid its broken tombs.
In the old days we should have heard a bell
Calling the monks before day broke to pray;
And when the day had broken on the ridge,
The crowing of its cocks.

YOUNG MAN.   Is there no house
Famous for sanctity or architectural beauty
In Clare or Kerry, or in all wide Connacht,
The enemy has not unroofed?

STRANGER.   Close to the altar
Broken by wind and frost and worn by time

Donough O'Brien has a tomb, a name in Latin.
He wore fine clothes and knew the secrets of women,
But he rebelled against the King of Thomond
And died in his youth.

YOUNG MAN.   And why should he rebel?
The King of Thomond was his rightful master.
It was men like Donough who made Ireland weak—
My curse on all that troop, and when I die
I'll leave my body, if I have any choice,
Far from his ivy-tod and his owl. Have those
Who, if your tale is true, work out a penance
Upon the mountain-top where I am to hide,
Come from the Abbey graveyard?

YOUNG GIRL.   They have not that luck,
But are more lonely; those that are buried there
Warred in the heat of the blood; if they were rebels
Some momentary impulse made them rebels,
Or the commandment of some petty king
Who hated Thomond. Being but common sinners,
No callers-in of the alien from oversea,
They and their enemies of Thomond's party
Mix in a brief dream-battle above their bones;
Or make one drove; or drift in amity;
Or in the hurry of the heavenly round
Forget their earthly names. These are alone,
Being accursed.

YOUNG MAN.   But if what seems is true
And there are more upon the other side
Than on this side of death, many a ghost
Must meet them face to face and pass the word
Even upon this grey and desolate hill.

YOUNG GIRL.   Until this hour no ghost or living man
Has spoken, though seven centuries have run
Since they, weary of life and of men's eyes,
Flung down their bones in some forgotten place,
Being accursed.

YOUNG MAN.   I have heard that there are souls
Who, having sinned after a monstrous fashion,

Take on them, being dead, a monstrous image
To drive the living, should they meet its face,
Crazy, and be a terror to the dead.

YOUNG GIRL.   But these
Were comely even in their middle life
And carry, now that they are dead, the image
Of their first youth, for it was in that youth
Their sin began.

YOUNG MAN.   I have heard of angry ghosts
Who wander in a wilful solitude.

YOUNG GIRL.   These have no thought but love; nor any joy
But that upon the instant when their penance
Draws to its height, and when two hearts are wrung
Nearest to breaking, if hearts of shadows break,
His eyes can mix with hers; nor any pang
That is so bitter as that double glance,
Being accursed.

YOUNG MAN.   But what is this strange penance—
That when their eyes have met can wring them most?

YOUNG GIRL.   Though eyes can meet, their lips can never meet.

YOUNG MAN.   And yet it seems they wander side by side.
But doubtless you would say that when lips meet
And have not living nerves, it is no meeting.

YOUNG GIRL.   Although they have no blood, or living nerves,
Who once lay warm and live the live-long night
In one another's arms, and know their part
In life, being now but of the people of dreams,
Is a dream's part; although they are but shadows,
Hovering between a thorn-tree and a stone,
Who have heaped up night on winged night; although
No shade however harried and consumed
Would change his own calamity for theirs,
Their manner of life were blessed could their lips
A moment meet; but when he has bent his head
Close to her head, or hand would slip in hand,
The memory of their crime flows up between
And drives them apart.

YOUNG MAN.   The memory of a crime—

He took her from a husband's house, it may be,
But does the penance for a passionate sin
Last for so many centuries?
YOUNG GIRL.   No, no;
The man she chose, the man she was chosen by,
Cared little and cares little from whose house
They fled towards dawn amid the flights of arrows,
Or that it was a husband's and a king's;
And how, if that were all, could she lack friends,
On crowded roads or on the unpeopled hill?
Helen herself had opened wide the door
Where night by night she dreams herself awake
And gathers to her breast a dreaming man.
YOUNG MAN.   What crime can stay so in the memory?
What crime can keep apart the lips of lovers
Wandering and alone?
YOUNG GIRL.   Her king and lover
Was overthrown in battle by her husband,
And for her sake and for his own, being blind
And bitter and bitterly in love, he brought
A foreign army from across the sea.
YOUNG MAN.   You speak of Diarmuid and Dervorgilla
Who brought the Norman in?
YOUNG GIRL.   Yes, yes, I spoke
Of that most miserable, most accursed pair
Who sold their country into slavery; and yet
They were not wholly miserable and accursed
If somebody of their race at last would say,
'I have forgiven them'.
YOUNG MAN.   O, never, never
Shall Diarmuid and Dervorgilla be forgiven.
YOUNG GIRL.   If some one of their race forgave at last
Lip would be pressed on lip.
YOUNG MAN.   O, never, never
Shall Diarmuid and Dervorgilla be forgiven.
You have told your story well, so well indeed
I could not help but fall into the mood
And for a while believe that it was true,

Or half believe; but better push on now.
The horizon to the east is growing bright.

[*They go round stage once. The Musicians play.*]

So here we're on the summit. I can see
The Aran Islands, Connemara Hills,
And Galway in the breaking light; there too
The enemy has toppled roof and gable,
And torn the panelling from ancient rooms;
What generations of old men had known
Like their own hands, and children wondered at,
Has boiled a trooper's porridge. That town had lain,
But for the pair that you would have me pardon,
Amid its gables and its battlements
Like any old admired Italian town;
For though we have neither coal, nor iron ore,
To make us wealthy and corrupt the air,
Our country, if that crime were uncommitted,
Had been most beautiful. Why do you dance?
Why do you gaze, and with so passionate eyes,
One on the other; and then turn away,
Covering your eyes, and weave it in a dance?
Who are you? what are you? you are not natural.

YOUNG GIRL.   Seven hundred years our lips have never met.

YOUNG MAN.   Why do you look so strangely at one another,
So strangely and so sweetly?

YOUNG GIRL.   Seven hundred years.

YOUNG MAN.   So strangely and so sweetly. All the ruin,
All, all their handiwork is blown away
As though the mountain air had blown it away
Because their eyes have met. They cannot hear,
Being folded up and hidden in their dance.
The dance is changing now. They have dropped their eyes,
They have covered up their eyes as though their hearts
Had suddenly been broken—never, never
Shall Diarmuid and Dervorgilla be forgiven.
They have drifted in the dance from rock to rock.
They have raised their hands as though to snatch the sleep
That lingers always in the abyss of the sky

Though they can never reach it. A cloud floats up
And covers all the mountain-head in a moment;
And now it lifts and they are swept away.

[*The Stranger and the Young Girl go out.*]

I had almost yielded and forgiven it all—
Terrible the temptation and the place!

[*The Musicians begin unfolding and folding a black cloth. The First Musician comes forward to the front of the stage, at the centre. He holds the cloth before him. The other two come one on either side and unfold it. They afterwards fold it up in the same way. While it is unfolded, the Young Man leaves the stage.*]

[*Songs for the unfolding and folding of the cloth*]

THE MUSICIANS [*singing*].

I

At the grey round of the hill
Music of a lost kingdom
Runs, runs and is suddenly still.
The winds out of Clare-Galway
Carry it: suddenly it is still.

I have heard in the night air
A wandering airy music;
And moidered in that snare
A man is lost of a sudden,
In that sweet wandering snare.

What finger first began
Music of a lost kingdom?
They dream that laughed in the sun.
Dry bones that dream are bitter,
They dream and darken our sun.

Those crazy fingers play
A wandering airy music;
Our luck is withered away,
And wheat in the wheat-ear withered,
And the wind blows it away.

II

My heart ran wild when it heard

The curlew cry before dawn
And the eddying cat-headed bird;
But now the night is gone.
I have heard from far below
The strong March birds a-crow.
Stretch neck and clap the wing,
Red cocks, and crow!

A PLAY IN ONE ACT

CHARACTERS

Chief Fisherman, Hakuryo
A Fisherman
A Tennin
Chorus

*The plot of the play Hagoromo, the Feather-mantle, is as follows: The priest finds
the Hagoromo, the magical feather-mantle of a Tennin, an aerial spirit or celestial
dancer, hanging upon a bough. She demands its return. He argues with her, and finally
promises to return it, if she will teach him her dance or part of it. She accepts the
offer. The Chorus explains the dance as symbolical of the daily changes of the moon.
The words about 'three, five, and fifteen' refer to the number of nights in the moon's
changes. In the finale, the Tennin is supposed to disappear like a mountain slowly
hidden in mist. The play shows the relation of the early Noh to the God-dance.*

HAKURYO.   Windy road of the waves by Miwo,
   Swift with ships, loud over steersmen's voices.
   Hakuryo, taker of fish, head of his house, dwells upon the barren pine-
waste of Miwo.
A FISHERMAN.   Upon a thousand heights had gathered the inexplicable
cloud. Swept by the rain, the moon is just come to light the high house.
   A clean and pleasant time surely. There comes the breath-colour of

spring; the waves rise in a line below the early mist; the moon is still delaying above, though we've no skill to grasp it. Here is a beauty to set the mind above itself.

CHORUS.   I shall not be out of memory
Of the mountain road by Kiyomi,
Nor of the parted grass by that bay,
Nor of the far seen pine-waste
Of Miwo of wheat stalks.

Let us go according to custom. Take hands against the wind here, for it presses the clouds and the sea. Those men who were going to fish are about to return without launching. Wait a little, is it not spring? will not the wind be quiet? This wind is only the voice of the lasting pine-trees, ready for stillness. See how the air is soundless, or would be, were it not for the waves. There now, the fishermen are putting out with even the smallest boats.

HAKURYO.   I am come to shore at Miwo-no; I disembark in Matsubara; I see all that they speak of on the shore. An empty sky with music, a rain of flowers, strange fragrance on every side; all these are no common things, nor is this cloak that hangs upon the pine-tree. As I approach to inhale its colour, I am aware of mystery. Its colour-smell is mysterious. I see that it is surely no common dress. I will take it now and return and make it treasure in my house, to show to the aged.

TENNIN.   That cloak belongs to some one on this side. What are you proposing to do with it?

HAKURYO.   This? this is a cloak picked up. I am taking it home, I tell you.

TENNIN.   That is a feather-mantle not fit for a mortal to bear,
Not easily wrested from the sky-traversing spirit,
Not easily taken or given.
I ask you to leave it where you found it.

HAKURYO.   How! Is the owner of this cloak a Tennin? So be it. In this downcast age I should keep it, a rare thing, and make it a treasure in the country, a thing respected. Then I should not return it.

TENNIN.   Pitiful, there is no flying without the cloak of feathers, no return through the ether. I pray you return me the mantle.

HAKURYO.   Just from hearing these words, I, Hakuryo, have gathered more and yet more force. You think, because I was too stupid to recognize it, that I shall be unable to take and keep hid the feather-robe, that I shall give it back for merely being told to stand and withdraw?

TENNIN.   A Tennin without her robe,

A bird without wings,
How shall she climb the air?

HAKURYO.   And this world would be a sorry place for her to dwell in?

TENNIN.   I am caught, I struggle, how shall I . . . ?

HAKURYO.   No, Hakuryo is not one to give back the robe.

TENNIN.   Power does not attain . . .

HAKURYO.   . . . to get back the robe. . . .

CHORUS.   Her coronet,* jewelled as with the dew of tears, even the flowers that decorated her hair, drooping and fading, the whole chain of weaknesses† of the dying Tennin can be seen actually before the eyes. Sorrow!

TENNIN.   I look into the flat of heaven, peering; the cloud-road is all hidden and uncertain; we are lost in the rising mist; I have lost the knowledge of the road. Strange, a strange sorrow!

CHORUS.   Enviable colour of breath, wonder of clouds that fade along the sky that was our accustomed dwelling; hearing the sky-bird, accustomed, and well accustomed, hearing the voices grow fewer, the wild geese fewer and fewer, along the highways of air, how deep her longing to return! Plover and seagull are on the waves in the offing. Do they go or do they return? She reaches out for the very blowing of the spring wind against heaven.

HAKURYO [to the Tennin].   What do you say? Now that I can see you in your sorrow, gracious, of heaven, I bend and would return you your mantle.

TENNIN.   It grows clearer. No, give it this side.

HAKURYO.   First tell me your nature, who are you, Tennin? Give payment with the dance of the Tennin, and I will return you your mantle.

TENNIN.   Readily and gladly, and then I return into heaven. You shall have what pleasure you will, and I will leave a dance here, a joy to be new among men and to be memorial dancing. Learn then this dance that can turn the palace of the moon. No, come here to learn it. For the sorrows of the world I will leave this new dancing with you for sorrowful people. But give me my mantle, I cannot do the dance rightly without it.

HAKURYO.   Not yet, for if you should get it, how do I know you'll not be

*Vide examples of state head-dress of kingfisher feathers in the South Kensington Museum.

†The chain of weaknesses, or the five ills, diseases of the Tennin: namely, the Tamakadzura withers; the Hagoromo is stained; sweat comes from the body; both eyes wink frequently; she feels very weary of her palace in heaven.

off to your palace without even beginning your dance, not even a measure?

TENNIN.   Doubt is of mortals; with us there is no deceit.

HAKURYO.   I am again ashamed. I give you your mantle.

CHORUS.   The young sprite now is arrayed, she assumes the curious mantle; watch how she moves in the dance of the rainbow-feathered garment.

HAKURYO.   The heavenly feather-robe moves in accord with the wind.

TENNIN.   The sleeves of flowers are being wet with the rain.

HAKURYO.   All three are doing one step.

CHORUS.   It seems that she dances.

> Thus was the dance of pleasure,
> Suruga dancing, brought to the sacred east.
> Thus was it when the lords of the everlasting
> Trod the world,
> They being of old our friends.
> Upon ten sides their sky is without limit,
> They have named it, on this account, the enduring.

TENNIN.   The jewelled axe takes up the eternal renewing, the palace of the moon-god is being renewed with the jewelled axe, and this is always recurring.

CHORUS [*commenting on the dance*].   The white kiromo, the black kiromo,
> Three, five into fifteen,
> The figure that the Tennin is dividing.
> There are heavenly nymphs, Amaotome,*
> One for each night of the month,
> And each with her deed assigned.

TENNIN.   I also am heaven-born and a maid, Amaotome. Of them there are many. This is the dividing of my body, that is fruit of the moon's tree, Katsura.† This is one part of our dance that I leave to you here in your world.

CHORUS.   The spring mist is widespread abroad; so perhaps the wild olive's flower will blossom in the infinitely unreachable moon. Her flowery head-ornament is putting on colour; this truly is sign of the spring. Not sky is here, but the beauty; and even here comes the heavenly, wonderful wind.

---

*Cf. 'Paradiso', xxiii. 25:
'Quale nei plenilunii sereni
Trivia ride tra le ninfe eterne.'
†A tree something like the laurel.

O blow shut the accustomed path of the clouds. O, you in the form of a maid, grant us the favour of your delaying. The pine-waste of Miwo puts on the colour of spring. The bay of Kiyomi lies clear before the snow upon Fuji. Are not all these presages of the spring? There are but few ripples beneath the piny wind. It is quiet along the shore. There is naught but a fence of jewels between the earth and the sky, and the gods within and without,* beyond and beneath the stars, and the moon unclouded by her lord, and we who are born of the sun. This alone intervenes, here where the moon is unshadowed, here in Nippon, the sun's field.

TENNIN. The plumage of heaven drops neither feather nor flame to its own diminution.

CHORUS.   Nor is this rock of earth overmuch worn by the brushing of that feather-mantle, the feathery skirt of the stars: rarely, how rarely. There is a magic song from the east, the voices of many and many: and flute and sho, filling the space beyond the cloud's edge, seven-stringed; dance filling and filling. The red sun blots on the sky the line of the colour-drenched mountains. The flowers rain in a gust; it is no racking storm that comes over this green moor, which is afloat, as it would seem, in these waves.

Wonderful is the sleeve of the white cloud, whirling such snow here.

TENNIN.   Plain of life, field of the sun, true foundation, great power!

CHORUS.   Hence and for ever this dancing shall be called 'a revel in the East.' Many are the robes thou hast, now of the sky's colour itself, and now a green garment.

SEMI-CHORUS.   And now the robe of mist, presaging spring, a colour-smell as this wonderful maiden's skirt—left, right, left! The rustling of flowers, the putting on of the feathery sleeve; they bend in air with the dancing.

SEMI-CHORUS.   Many are the joys in the east. She who is the colour-person of the moon takes her middle-night in the sky. She marks her three fives with this dancing, as a shadow of all fulfilments. The circled vows are at full. Give the seven jewels of rain and all of the treasure, you who go from us. After a little time, only a little time, can the mantle be upon the wind that was spread over Matsubara or over Ashitaka the mountain, though the clouds lie in its heaven like a plain awash with sea. Fuji is gone; the great peak of Fuji is blotted out little by little. It melts into the upper mist. In this way she (the Tennin) is lost to sight.

*'Within and without', gei, gu, two parts of the temple.

A Play in Two Acts, by Motokiyo

CHARACTERS

The Waki, *a priest*
The Shite, or Hero, *ghost of the lover*
Tsure, *ghost of the woman; they have both been*
  long dead, and have not been united
A Chorus

Part First

WAKI.   There never was anybody heard of Mt. Shinobu but had a kindly feeling for it; so I, like any other priest that might want to know a little bit about each one of the provinces, may as well be walking up here along the much-travelled road.

I have not yet been about the east country, but now I have set my mind to go as far as the earth goes, and why shouldn't I, after all? seeing that I go about with my heart set upon no particular place whatsoever, and with no other man's flag in my hand, no more than a cloud has. It is a flag of the night I see coming down upon me. I wonder now, would the sea be that way, or the little place Kefu that they say is stuck down against it.

SHITE AND TSURE.   Times out of mind am I here setting up this bright branch, this silky wood with the charms painted in it as fine as the web you'd get in the grass-cloth of Shinobu, that they'd be still selling you in this mountain.

The 'Nishikigi' are wands used as a love-charm. 'Hosonuno' is the name of a local cloth which the woman weaves.

147

SHITE [to Tsure]. Tangled, we are entangled. Whose fault was it, dear? tangled up as the grass patterns are tangled in this coarse cloth, or as the little Mushi that lives on and chirrups in dried seaweed. We do not know where are to-day our tears in the undergrowth o this eternal wilderness. We neither wake nor sleep, and passing our nights in a sorrow which is in the end a vision, what are these scenes of spring to us? this thinking in sleep, of some one who has no thought of you, is it more than a dream? and yet surely it is the natural way of love. In our hearts there is much and in our bodies nothing, and we do nothing at all, and only the waters of the river of tears flow quickly.

CHORUS.   Narrow is the cloth of Kefu, but wild is that river, that torrent
of the hills, between the beloved and the bride.

The cloth she had woven is faded, the thousand one hundred nights were
night-trysts watched out in vain.

WAKI [not recognizing the nature of the speakers].   Strange indeed, seeing
these town-people here,

They seem like man and wife,

And the lady seems to be holding something

Like a cloth woven of feathers,

While he has a staff or a wooden sceptre

Beautifully ornate.

Both of these things are strange;

In any case, I wonder what they call them.

TSURE.   This is a narrow cloth called 'Hosonuno,'

It is just the breadth of the loom.

SHITE.   And this is merely wood painted,

And yet the place is famous because of these things.

Would you care to buy them from us?

WAKI.   Yes, I know that the cloth of this place and the lacquers are famous things. I have already heard of their glory, and yet I still wonder why
they have such great reputation.

TSURE.   Well now, that's a disappointment. Here they call the wood
'Nishikigi,' and the woven stuff 'Hosonuno', and yet you come saying that
you have never heard why, and never heard the story. Is it reasonable?

SHITE.   No, no, that is reasonable enough. What can people be expected
to know of these affairs when it is more than they can do to keep abreast of
their own?

BOTH [to the Priest].   Ah well, you look like a person who has abandoned
the world; it is reasonable enough that you should not know the worth

of wands and cloths with love's signs painted upon them, with love's marks painted and dyed.

WAKI.   That is a fine answer. And you would tell me then that Nishikigi and Hosonuno are names bound over with love?

SHITE.   They are names in love's list surely. Every day for a year, for three years come to their full, the wands, Nishikigi, were set up, until there were a thousand in all. And they are in song in your time, and will be. 'Chidzuka' they call them.

TSURE.   These names are surely a byword.
As the cloth Hosonuno is narrow of weft,
More narrow than the breast,
We call by this name any woman
Whose breasts are hard to come nigh to.
It is a name in books of love.

SHITE.   'Tis a sad name to look back on.

TSURE.   A thousand wands were in vain.
A sad name, set in a story.

SHITE.   A seed pod void of the seed,
We had no meeting together.

TSURE.   Let him read out the story.

CHORUS.   At last they forget, they forget.
The wands are no longer offered,
The custom is faded away.
The narrow cloth of Kefu
Will not meet over the breast.
'Tis the story of Hosonuno,
This is the tale:
These bodies, having no weft,
Even now are not come together.
Truly a shameful story,
A tale to bring shame on the gods.
Names of love,
Now for a little spell,
For a faint charm only,
For a charm as slight as the binding together
Of pine-flakes in Iwashiro,
And for saying a wish over them about sunset,
We return, and return to our lodging.
The evening sun leaves a shadow.

WAKI. Go on, tell out all the story.

SHITE. There is an old custom of this country. We make wands of mediation and deck them with symbols and set them before a gate when we are suitors.

TSURE. And we women take up a wand of the man we would meet with, and let the others lie, although a man might come for a hundred nights, it may be, or for a thousand nights in three years, till there were a thousand wands here in the shade of this mountain. We know the funeral cave of such a man, one who had watched out the thousand nights; a bright cave, for they buried him with all his wands. They have named it the 'Cave of the many charms.'

WAKI. I will go to that love-cave,

It will be a tale to take back to my village.

Will you show me my way there?

SHITE. So be it, I will teach you the path.

TSURE. Tell him to come over this way.

BOTH. Here are the pair of them

Going along before the traveller.

CHORUS. We have spent the whole day until dusk

Pushing aside the grass

From the overgrown way at Kefu,

And we are not come to the cave.

O you there, cutting grass on the hill,

Please set your mind on this matter.

'You'd be asking where the dew is

'While the frost's lying here on the road.

'Who'd tell you that now?'

Very well, then, don't tell us,

But be sure we will come to the cave.

SHITE. There's a cold feel in the autumn.

Night comes. . . .

CHORUS. And storms; trees giving up their leaf,

Spotted with sudden showers.

Autumn! our feet are clogged

In the dew-drenched, entangled leaves.

The perpetual shadow is lonely,

The mountain shadow is lying alone.

The owl cries out from the ivies

That drag their weight on the pine.

Among the orchids and chrysanthemum flowers
The hiding fox is now lord of that love-cave,
Nishidzuka,
That is dyed like the maple's leaf.
They have left us this thing for a saying.
That pair have gone into the cave. [*Sign for the exit of Shite and Tsure.*]

PART SECOND

The Waki has taken the posture of sleep. His respectful visit to the cave is beginning to have its effect.

WAKI [*restless*].   It seems that I cannot sleep
For the length of a pricket's horn.
Under October wind, under pines, under night!
I will do service to Butsu.

[*He performs the gestures of a ritual.*]

TSURE.   Aïe, honoured priest!
You do not dip twice in the river
Beneath the same tree's shadow
Without bonds in some other life.
Hear soothsay,
Now is there meeting between us,
Between us who were until now
In life and in after-life kept apart.
A dream-bridge over wild grass,
Over the grass I dwell in.
O honoured! do not awake me by force.
I see that the law is perfect.

SHITE [*supposedly invisible*].   It is a good service you have done, sir,
A service that spreads in two worlds,
And binds up an ancient love
That was stretched out between them.
I had watched for a thousand days.
I give you largess,
For this meeting is under a difficult law.
And now I will show myself in the form of Nishikigi.
I will come out now for the first time in colour.

CHORUS.   The three years are over and past:
All that is but an old story.

SHITE.   To dream under dream we return.
　　Three years. . . . And the meeting comes now!
　　This night has happened over and over,
　　And only now comes the tryst.
CHORUS.   Look there to the cave
　　Beneath the stems of the Suzuki.
　　From under the shadow of the love-grass,
　　See, see how they come forth and appear
　　For an instant. . . . Illusion!
SHITE.   There is at the root of hell
　　No distinction between princes and commons;
　　Wretched for me! 'tis the saying.
WAKI.   Strange, what seemed so very old a cave
　　Is all glittering-bright within,
　　Like the flicker of fire.
　　It is like the inside of a house.
　　They are setting up a loom,
　　And heaping up charm-sticks. No,
　　The hangings are out of old time.
　　Is it illusion, illusion?
TSURE.   Our hearts have been in the dark of the falling snow,
　　We have been astray in the flurry.
　　You should tell better than we
　　How much is illusion,
　　You who are in the world.
　　We have been in the whirl of those who are fading.
SHITE.   Indeed in old times Narihira said
　　(And he has vanished with the years),
　　'Let a man who is in the world tell the fact.'
　　It is for you, traveller,
　　To say how much is illusion.
WAKI.   Let it be a dream, or a vision,
　　Or what you will, I care not.
　　Only show me the old times over-past and snowed under;
　　Now, soon, while the night lasts.
SHITE.   Look, then, for the old times are shown,
　　Faint as the shadow-flower shows in the grass that bears it;
　　And you've but a moon for lanthorn.

TSURE.   The woman has gone into the cave.
  She sets up her loom there
  For the weaving of Hosonuno,
  Thin as the heart of Autumn.
SHITE.   The suitor for his part, holding his charm-sticks,
  Knocks on a gate which was barred.
TSURE.   In old time he got back no answer,
  No secret sound at all
  Save . . .
SHITE.   . . . the sound of the loom.
TSURE.   It was a sweet sound like katydids and crickets,
  A thin sound like the Autumn.
SHITE.   It was what you would hear any night.
TSURE.   Kiri.
SHITE.   Hatari.
TSURE.   Cho.
SHITE.   Cho.
CHORUS [*mimicking the sound of crickets*].   Kiri, hatari, cho, cho,
  Kiri, hatari, cho, cho.
  The cricket sews on at his old rags,
  With all the new grass in the field; sho,
  Churr, isho, like the whirr of a loom: churr.
CHORUS [*antistrophe*].   Let be, they make grass-cloth in Kefu,
  Kefu, the land's end, matchless in the world.
SHITE.   That is an old custom, truly,
  But this priest would look on the past.
CHORUS.   The good priest himself would say:
  Even if we weave the cloth, Hosonuno,
  And set up the charm-sticks
  For a thousand, a hundred nights;
  Even then our beautiful desire will not pass,
  Nor fade nor die out.
SHITE.   Even to-day the difficulty of our meeting is remembered,
  And is remembered in song.
CHORUS.   That we may acquire power,
  Even in our faint substance.
  We will show forth even now,
  And though it be but in a dream,

Our form of repentance.

[*Explaining the movement of the Shite and Tsure.*]

There he is carrying wands,
And she had no need to be asked.
See her within the cave,
With a cricket-like noise of weaving.
The grass-gates and the hedge are between them,
That is a symbol.
Night has already come on.

[*Now explaining the thoughts of the man's spirit.*]

Love's thoughts are heaped high within him,
As high as the charm-sticks,
As high as the charm-sticks, once coloured,
Now fading, lie heaped in this cave;
And he knows of their fading. He says:
I lie, a body, unknown to any other man,
Like old wood buried in moss.
It were a fit thing
That I should stop thinking the love-thoughts,
The charm-sticks fade and decay,
And yet,
The rumour of our love
Takes foot, and moves through the world.
We had no meeting.
But tears have, it seems, brought out a bright blossom
Upon the dyed tree of love.

SHITE.   Tell me, could I have foreseen
Or known what a heap of my writings
Should lie at the end of her shaft-bench?

CHORUS.   A hundred nights and more
Of twisting, encumbered sleep,
And now they make it a ballad,
Not for one year or for two only,
But until the days lie deep
As the sand's depth at Kefu.
Until the year's end is red with autumn,
Red like these love-wands,
A thousand nights are in vain.
I, too, stand at this gate-side:

You grant no admission, you do not show yourself
Until I and my sleeves are faded.
By the dew-like gemming of tears upon my sleeve,
Why will you grant no admission?
And we all are doomed to pass
You, and my sleeves and my tears.
And you did not even know when three years had come to an end.
Cruel, ah, cruel!
The charm-sticks . . .

SHITE.   . . . were set up a thousand times;
Then, now, and for always.

CHORUS.   Shall I ever at last see into that secret bride-room, which no
    other sight has traversed?

SHITE.   Happy at last and well-starred,
    Now comes the eve of betrothal;
    We meet for the wine-cup.

CHORUS.   How glorious the sleeves of the dance,
    That are like snow-whirls!

SHITE.   Tread out the dance.

CHORUS.   Tread out the dance and bring music.
    This dance is for Nishikigi.

SHITE.   This dance is for the evening plays,
    And for the weaving.

CHORUS.   For the tokens between lover and lover:
    It is a reflecting in the wine-cup.

CHORUS.   Ari-aki,
    The dawn!
    Come, we are out of place;
    Let us go ere the light comes,

[To the Waki.]

We ask you, do not awake,
We all will wither away.
The wands and this cloth of a dream.
Now you will come out of sleep,
You tread the border and nothing
Awaits you: no, all this will wither away.
There is nothing here but this cave in the field's midst.
To-day's wind moves in the pines;
A wild place, unlit, and unfilled.

BIBLIOGRAPHY

WORKS OF W. B. YEATS

Autobiographies. New York: Macmillan, 1938.

Autobiographies. London: Macmillan, 1961.

Beltaine: An Occasional Publication (ed). London: At the Sign of the Unicorn, 1899–1900.

The Celtic Twilight. London: Lawrence & Bullen, 1893.

Certain Noble Plays of Japan, chosen and finished by Ezra Pound (introduction). Dublin: Cuala Press, 1916.

The Collected Plays of W. B. Yeats. 2nd ed. London: Macmillan, 1952.

The Collected Poems of W. B. Yeats. New York: Macmillan, 1949.

The Cutting of an Agate. London: Macmillan, 1919.

Dramatis Personae. New York: Macmillan, 1936.

Essays. New York: Macmillan, 1924.

Explorations. London: Macmillan, 1962.

Fairy and Folk Tales of the Irish Peasantry (ed.). London: W. Scott, 1888.

If I Were Four and Twenty. Dublin: Cuala Press, 1940.

Last Poems and Plays. New York: Macmillan, 1940.

Mythologies. London: Macmillan, 1959.

A Packet for Ezra Pound. Dublin: Cuala Press, 1929.

Plays and Controversies. New York: Macmillan, 1924.

Plays in Prose and Verse. New York: Macmillan, 1930.

The Ten Principal Upanishads (Purohit Swami and, trans.). London: Faber & Faber, 1937.

Wheels and Butterflies. New York: Macmillan, 1934.

A Vision. Rev. ed. London: Macmillan, 1962.

WORKS ON THE NOH

Beck, L. Adams. "The Ghost-Plays of Japan." *Atlantic Monthly,* January 1923.

Ernst, Earle, and Haar, Francis. *Japanese Theatre in Highlight*. Rutland, Vt., and Tokyo: Charles E. Tuttle, 1954.

Fenollosa, Ernest, and Pound, Ezra. *'Noh' or Accomplishment: A Study of the Classical Stage of Japan*. London: Macmillan, 1916.

Ishibashi, Hiro. "W. B. Yeats and the Noh." Doctoral dissertation. Tokyo: Keio University, 1956.

Japanese Classics Translation Committee. *The Noh Drama: Ten Plays Selected and Translated from the Japanese*. UNESCO Collection of Representative Works: Japanese Series. Rutland, Vt., and Tokyo: Charles E. Tuttle, 1955.

Noguchi, Yone, trans. *Ten Kiogen in English*. Tokyo: Tozaisha, 1907.

Pound, Ezra, and Fenollosa, Ernest. *The Classic Noh Theatre of Japan*. New York: New Directions, 1959.

Qamber, Akhtar. "The Noh: Classical Dance Drama of the Shogunate Period." *Natya* 4 (1963), pp. 77–83. New Delhi: Bharatiya Natya Sangh.

Sadler, A. L. *Japanese Plays: No—Kyogen—Kabuki*. Sydney: Angus & Robertson, 1934.

Society for International Cultural Relations (Kokusai Bunka Shinkokai). *The Noh Drama*. Tokyo: Kokusai Bunka Shinkokai, 1937.

Stopes, Marie C., and Sakurai, Joji. *Plays of Old Japan: The Nō*. London: William Heinemann, 1913.

Suzuki, Beatrice Lane. *Japanese Nō Plays*. London: John Murray, 1932.

———, trans. *Nōgaku: Japanese Nō Plays*. New York: n.p., 1932.

Waley, Arthur. *The No Plays of Japan*. London: Allen & Unwin, 1921.

Wells, Henry W. *The Classical Drama of the Orient*. Bombay: Asia Publishing House, 1965.

Zeami, Motokiyo. *Birds of Sorrow*. Translated by Meredith Weatherby and Bruce Rogers. Tokyo: Obunsha, 1947.

GENERAL BIBLIOGRAPHY

Books

Ansari, A. A. *Arrows of Intellect: A Study in William Blake's Gospel of the Imagination*. Aligarh, India: Naya Kitabghar, 1965.

Bax, Clifford, ed. *Florence Farr, Bernard Shaw, W. B. Yeats: Letters*. London: Home & Van Thal, 1946.

Beerbohm, Max. *The Works of Max Beerbohm*. New York: Charles Scribner's Sons, 1896.

Bodkin, Maud. *Archetypal Patterns in Poetry*. London: Oxford University Press, 1934.

Bose, A. C. *Three Mystic Poets*. Kohlapur, India: School and College Bookstall, 1945.

Brill, A. A., ed. and trans. *The Basic Writings of Sigmund Freud*. New York: Modern Library, 1937.

Brooks, Cleanth. *The Hidden God: Studies in Hemingway, Faulkner, Yeats, Eliot, and Warren.* New Haven, Conn.: Yale University Press, 1963.

———. *The Well Wrought Urn: Studies in the Structure of Poetry.* London: Dennis Doleson, 1960.

Bushrui, S. B. *Yeats' Verse Plays: The Revisions, 1900–1910.* London: Oxford University Press, 1966.

Clark, David R. *W. B. Yeats and the Theatre of Desolate Reality.* Dublin: Dolmen Press, 1965.

Cohen, J. M. *A History of Western Literature.* London: Cassell, 1961.

Drew, Elizabeth. *T. S. Eliot: The Design of His Poetry.* New York: Charles Scribner's Sons, 1949.

Ellis-Fermor, Una. *The Irish Dramatic Movement.* London: Methuen, 1939.

Ellmann, Richard. *The Identity of Yeats.* London: Macmillan, 1954.

———. *Yeats: The Man and the Masks.* New York: Macmillan, 1948.

Empson, William. *Seven Types of Ambiguity.* London: Chatto & Windus, 1947.

Enright, D. J. *The World of Dew.* London: Secker & Warburg, 1955.

Fay, Gerard. *The Abbey Theatre: Cradle of Genius.* London: Hollis & Carter, 1958.

Fraser, George S. *W. B. Yeats.* Rev. ed. London: Longmans Green, 1962.

Frazer, James. *The Golden Bough.* London: Macmillan, 1950.

Freud, Sigmund. *The Interpretation of Dreams.* London: Allen & Unwin, 1932.

Gibbon, Monk. *The Masterpiece and the Man: Yeats As I Know Him.* London: Rupert Hart-Davis, 1959.

Gogarty, Oliver St. John. *William Butler Yeats: A Memoir.* Dublin: Dolmen Press, 1963.

Gregory, Augusta. *Cuchulain of Muirthemne.* London: John Murray, 1902.

———. *Gods and Fighting Men.* London: John Murray, 1910.

Gwynn, Stephen, ed. *Scattering Branches: Tributes to the Memory of W. B. Yeats.* New York: Macmillan, 1940.

Hall, James, and Steinmann, Martin, eds. *The Permanence of Yeats.* New York: Macmillan, 1950.

Henn, Thomas R. *The Lonely Tower.* London: Methuen, 1950.

Hirst, Désirée. *Hidden Riches: Traditional Symbolism from the Renaissance to Blake.* London: Eyre & Spottiswoode, 1964.

Hone, Joseph. *W. B. Yeats: 1865–1939.* New York: Macmillan, 1943.

———. *William Butler Yeats: The Poet in Contemporary Ireland.* Dublin: Mansel, 1916.

Hough, Graham. *The Last Romantics.* London: Duckworth, 1949.

Hughes, Glenn. *Imagism and the Imagists.* Stanford, Calif.: Stanford University Press, 1931.

Hymen, Stanley Edgar. *Armed Vision.* New York: n.p., 1948.

Jeffares, A. Norman. *W. B. Yeats: Man and Poet.* London: Routledge & Kegan Paul, 1949.

———. *W. B. Yeats: The Poems.* London: Edward Arnold, 1961.

————, and Cross, K. G. W., eds. *In Excited Reverie: A Centenary Tribute to William Butler Yeats, 1865–1939*. London and New York: Macmillan, 1965.

Joyce, James. *Ulysess*. New York: Modern Library, Random House, 1934.

Kermode, Frank. *Romantic Image*. London: Routledge & Kegan Paul, 1961.

Koch, Vivienne. *W. B. Yeats: Tragic Phase*. London: Routledge & Kegan Paul, 1951.

Krans, Horatio Sheafe. *William Butler Yeats and the Irish Literary Revival*. New York: McClure Phillips, 1904.

Langer, Susanne K. *Philosophy in a New Key*. New York: New American Library, 1948 (orig. pub. Cambridge, Mass.: Harvard University Press, 1942).

Legouis, Emile, and Cazamian, Louis. *A History of English Literature*. Rev. ed. London: J. M. Dent & Sons, 1960.

Lewis, C. S. *English Literature in the Sixteenth Century*. London: Oxford University Press, 1944.

MacNeice, Louis. *The Poetry of W. B. Yeats*. New York: Oxford University Press, 1941.

Menon, V. K. N. *The Development of William Butler Yeats*. Edinburgh: Oliver & Boyd, 1942.

Mullahy, Patrick. *Oedipus Myth and Complex: A Review of Psychoanalytic Theory*. New York: Hermitage Press, 1948.

Nelson, B., ed. *Freud and the Twentieth Century*. London: Allen & Unwin, 1958.

O'Donnell, J. P. *Sailing to Byzantium: A Study in the Development of the Later Style and Symbolism in the Poetry of W. B. Yeats*. Cambridge, Mass.: Harvard University Press, 1939.

Plotinus. *The Six Enneads*. Translated by Stephen MacKenna and B. S. Page. Great Books of the Western World, edited by Robert Maynard Hutchins. Chicago: Encyclopaedia Britannica, University of Chicago Press, 1952.

Rajan, Balachandra. *W. B. Yeats: A Critical Introduction*. London: Hutchinson University Library, 1965.

Reischauer, Edwin O. *Japan Past and Present*. Tokyo: Charles E. Tuttle, 1959.

Robinson, Lennox. *Ireland's Abbey Theatre: A History, 1899–1951*. London: Sidgwick & Jackson, 1951.

————, ed. *Lady Gregory's Journal*. New York: Macmillan, 1947.

Rudd, Margaret E. *Divided Image*. London: Routledge & Kegan Paul, 1953.

Scully, James. *Modern Poets on Modern Poetry*. London: Fontana Library, 1966.

Stauffer, Donald A. *The Golden Nightingale*. New York: Macmillan, 1949.

Symons, Arthur, ed. *The Savoy*. London: Leonard Smithers, 1896.

————. *The Symbolist Movement in Literature*. New York: E. P. Dutton, 1908.

Tindall, William York. *Forces in Modern British Literature: 1885–1946*. New York: Alfred A. Knopf, 1947.

————. *Forces in Modern British Literature: 1885–1956*. New York: Vintage Books, 1956.

Unterecker, John. *A Reader's Guide to William Butler Yeats*. London: Thames & Hudson, 1959.

―――. ed. *Yeats*. Englewood Cliffs, N. J.: Prentice-Hall, 1963.

Ure, Peter. *Yeats the Playwright*. London: Routledge & Kegan Paul, 1963.

Weston, Jessie L. *From Ritual to Romance*. London: D. Van Nostrand, 1961.

Weygandt, Cornelius. *Irish Plays and Playwrights*. New York: Houghton Mifflin, 1913.

Wilson, Edmund. *Axel's Castle*. New York: Charles Scribner's Sons, 1931.

Wilson, F. A. C. *W. B. Yeats and Tradition*. London: Victor Gollancz, 1958.

Yeats, John Butler. *Letters to His Son W. B. Yeats and Others*. Edited by Joseph Hone. New York: E. P. Dutton, 1946.

Zwerdling, Alex. *Yeats and the Heroic Ideal*. London: Peter Owen, 1966.

Periodicals

Fay, Gerard. "The Abbey Theatre." *Ireland,* July-August 1966, pp. 28–32.

Firkins, O. W. "Four Plays for Dancers by W. B. Yeats." *The Yale Review: A National Quarterly,* new series 12 (October 1922), p. 193.

" 'Four Plays for Dancers' by Yeats." *The Times Literary Supplement,* December 15, 1921, p. 840.

Keene, Donald. "Conventions of the Nō Drama." *Columbia Forum: A Quarterly Journal of Fact and Opinion,* vol. 13, no. 2 (summer 1970), pp. 30–32.

Murphy, Gerard. "Douglas Hyde." *Irish Quarterly Review* 38 (September 1949).

The Nation 114 (May 10, 1922), p. 573.

The Nation & Atlantic 30 (February 11, 1922), p. 730.

The New Republic 30 (March 14, 1922), p. 84.

The New York Times, January 20, 1922.

Pitkin, William. "Stage Designs, Masks and Costumes for Plays of W. B. Yeats." With introductory notes by Sherman Conrad. *Bard Review,* n.d., pp. 93–110.

Raine, Kathleen. Review of *Yeats: The Man and the Masks,* by Richard Ellmann. *The New Statesman & Nation* 38 (December 10, 1949), p. 700.

Theatre Arts, January 1922, p. 79.

Wilson, Edmund. "The Poetry of Mr. W. B. Yeats." *Freeman's Journal* 5 (March 1922).

"The Wizardry of Mr. Yeats: 'Four Plays for Dancers.' " *The Saturday Review of Literature* 132 (December 3, 1921), p. 643.

The "weathermark" identifies this book as a production of John Weatherhill, Inc., publishers of fine books on Asia and the Pacific. Supervising editor, book designer, and typographer: Suzanne Trumbull. Production supervisor: Yutaka Shimoji. Composition: Samhwa Printing Company, Seoul. Printing: Kenkyusha Printing Company, Tokyo. Binding: Okamoto Binderies, Tokyo. The typeface used is Monotype Perpetua, with Perpetua for display.